The Memorialization of Genocide

Divided societies, tormented pasts, and unrepentant perpetrators. Why are some countries more intent on vanquishing uncomfortable pasts than others? How do public and often unsightly attempts at memorialization both fail the victims and valorize their oppressors?

This book offers fresh and original perspectives on dictatorship, fascism and victimization from the bloodiest decades in Europe's, Australia's and Central America's colonial and modern history. Chapters include analyses of Francoist memorials in Spain, assessments of the El Mozote massacre in El Salvador, the forgetting of frontier colonial violence in Tasmania, Romania's treatment of its Roma populations in the midst of Holocaust memorialization in Bucharest's urban development, and whether or not the Holocaust continues to serve as an instructional model or impossible aspiration for cross-cultural genocide memorialization strategies. In an era of ongoing political, ethnic and religious conflict, and unrepentant insurgent activity around the world, this collection reminds readers that genocidal actions, wherever and whenever they occurred, must be held to account by more than rhetoric and concrete memory.

This book was originally published as a special issue of the *Journal of Genocide Research*.

Simone Gigliotti teaches in the History Programme at Victoria University of Wellington, New Zealand. She is the author of books, chapters and articles on the Holocaust and comparative genocide studies. Her current research projects focus on film activism and DPs in postwar Europe and Holocaust transmigrations in South-East Asia.

The Memorialization of Genocide

Edited by
Simone Gigliotti

Routledge
Taylor & Francis Group
LONDON AND NEW YORK

First published 2016 by Routledge

2 Park Square, Milton Park, Abingdon, Oxon OX14 4RN
711 Third Avenue, New York, NY 10017, USA

Routledge is an imprint of the Taylor & Francis Group, an informa business

First issued in paperback 2017

British Library Cataloguing in Publication Data
A catalogue record for this book is available from the British Library

ISBN 13: 978-1-138-93211-1 (hbk)
ISBN 13: 978-1-138-09901-2 (pbk)

Typeset in Times New Roman
by RefineCatch Limited, Bungay, Suffolk

Publisher's Note
The publisher accepts responsibility for any inconsistencies that may have arisen during the conversion of this book from journal articles to book chapters, namely the possible inclusion of journal terminology.

Contents

Citation Information

The chapters in this book were originally published in the *Journal of Genocide Research*, volume 16, issue 4 (December 2014). When citing this material, please use the original page numbering for each article, as follows:

Introduction
The memorialization of genocide
Simone Gigliotti
Journal of Genocide Research, volume 16, issue 4 (December 2014) pp. 421–422

Chapter 1
Thinking comparatively about genocide memorialization
Rebecca Jinks
Journal of Genocide Research, volume 16, issue 4 (December 2014) pp. 423–440

Chapter 2
Memorializing colonial genocide in Britain: the case of Tasmania
Tom Lawson
Journal of Genocide Research, volume 16, issue 4 (December 2014) pp. 441–461

Chapter 3
Site of memory and dismemory: the Valley of the Fallen in Spain
Andrea Hepworth
Journal of Genocide Research, volume 16, issue 4 (December 2014) pp. 463–485

Chapter 4
Holocaust commemoration in Romania: Roma and the contested politics of memory and memorialization
Michelle Kelso and Daina S. Eglitis
Journal of Genocide Research, volume 16, issue 4 (December 2014) pp. 487–511

Chapter 5

Revisiting the El Mozote massacre: memory and politics in postwar El Salvador
Rafael Alarcón Medina and Leigh Binford
Journal of Genocide Research, volume 16, issue 4 (December 2014) pp. 513–533

Notes on Contributors

Rafael Alarcón Medina is a Postdoctoral Researcher in the Postgraduate Program in Architecture and Urbanism at the Universidade Federal de Minas Gerais, Belo Horizonte, Brazil. His current research explores the relations between digital media, urban space production and the social logics of capitalist domination in the favelas of Belo Horizonte in Brazil.

Leigh Binford is Chair of the Sociology and Anthropology Department at the College of Staten Island, City University of New York, USA. He has carried out fieldwork in Mexico, El Salvador and Canada, focusing on rural social economies, peasantries, international migration and human rights.

Daina S. Eglitis is Associate Professor of Sociology and International Affairs at George Washington University, Washington, D.C., USA. Her research examines the social dimensions of post-communist transformations in East and Central Europe. Her articles have appeared in *Acta Sociologica*, *Cultural Sociology*, *Europe-Asia Studies*, *Nationalities Papers*, and *Slavic Review*, among others. She is a two-time Fulbright Fellow and a 2014–2015 fellowship recipient at the US Holocaust Memorial Museum. She is also the author of *Imagining the Nation: history, modernity, and revolution in Latvia*, and a co-author of *Discover Sociology*.

Simone Gigliotti teaches in the History Programme at Victoria University of Wellington, New Zealand. She is the author of books, chapters and articles on the Holocaust and comparative genocide studies. Her current research projects focus on film activism and DPs in postwar Europe and Holocaust transmigrations in South-East Asia.

Andrea Hepworth has recently completed her PhD at Victoria University of Wellington, New Zealand. Her interdisciplinary comparative research project focused on current debates in Spain and Germany about how to deal with each country's highly controversial twentieth-century history, based on case studies of memorial sites in both countries. Her interests lie in twentieth-century European comparative cultural studies, memory studies, the intergenerational transmission of traumatic memories and the legacy of traumatic pasts on the present.

Rebecca Jinks received her PhD in 2013 from Royal Holloway, University of London, UK, and her thesis was entitled 'Representing genocide: the Holocaust as paradigm?'

She has written a number of articles on comparative representations of genocide in the press, and her next project explores the rescue of Armenian women who had been 'absorbed' into Muslim homes by humanitarian organizations and the League of Nations during the genocide.

Michelle Kelso is Assistant Professor of Human Services, Sociology and International Affairs at George Washington University, Washington, D.C., USA. Her research interests include collective memory, the Holocaust, education and migration. She has been the recipient of several prestigious national awards, including two Fulbright fellowships to Romania and a Charles H. Revson Fellowship at the US Holocaust Memorial Museum. She also made a well-received documentary film in 2005, entitled 'Hidden Sorrows: the persecution of Romanian Gypsies during WWII', which has screened in several countries, at numerous film festivals, and aired on national television channels.

Tom Lawson is Associate Dean (Academic) and Professor of History in the Faculty of Arts, Design and Social Sciences at Northumbria University, Newcastle, UK. He is the co-editor of the journal *Holocaust Studies: A Journal of Culture and History*, and is the author and editor of several books. These include *The Last Man: a British genocide in Tasmania* (2014); *Debates on the Holocaust* (2010); *The Memory of the Holocaust in Australia* (edited with James Jordan, 2008); and *The Church of England and the Holocaust* (2006).

INTRODUCTION

The memorialization of genocide

SIMONE GIGLIOTTI

The origin of this special issue, 'The memorialization of genocide', emerged from a *Journal of Genocide Research* workshop held at the Wiener Library, London, in November 2012. The journal editors invited scholars whose research explores the practices, places and politics of genocide memorialization in Europe, Africa, Latin America and South-East Asia. The articles published in this issue represent a selection of those papers (Rebecca Jinks, Tom Lawson, Michelle Kelso and Rafael Alarcón Medina) and also commissioned new articles (Andrea Hepworth). A few presenters took on co-authors to develop their papers into research articles (Kelso and Alarcón Medina). Not all case studies presented in this issue might be considered 'clear cut' cases of genocide. Indeed, perhaps residually significant issues relate to violence and the emotional and social claims and investments in mourning it, and forgetting it. Related, too, is the unsettlement that comes with labouring over personal memory and its transformations into concrete form, or its humble markings in landscapes, hills and buildings.

As these articles suggest, there are few clearer markers of the politicization of the past than in memorial building, shifting and dismantling. In 'Thinking comparatively about genocide memorialization', Rebecca Jinks offers a cogent outline of the evolution of memorialization practices as a comparative phenomenon, drawing examples from the Holocaust, Rwanda, Armenia and Cambodia. In line with recent scholarship to question the importance of the Holocaust as a paradigmatic marker of genocide, her article works as a foundation for rethinking the local histories and geographies of genocide memorialization in museum and public sites. The positive touristic and human rights outcomes associated with the increase in memorial building are increasingly promoted as evidence of governments' and other stakeholder groups' achievements in stabilizing extreme narratives of violence in post-conflict and post-genocide societies.

Tom Lawson's 'Memorializing colonial genocide in Britain: the case of Tasmania' offers an engaging interpretation of the British Empire looking back at its dark past, not flinching at its role in commissioning atrocities and genocide in

Tasmania. Lawson suggests that Britain, as a 'perpetrator' society, has not ignored these colonial atrocities but rather has constructed positive narratives about this history. The article is, as Lawson notes, a study of British cultural engagement with Tasmania in art, opera, museums (display of Aboriginal human remains as trophies of conquest) and literature, an engagement that normalized the destructive impact of British settlement as a progress narrative. Rather than embarking on some form of apology, as offered by previous British governments in relation to the slave trade and slavery in the Caribbean, Lawson suggests that Britons have been socialized, and successfully so, to 'master the past'.

The dysfunction and displacement that surround the 'political lives of dead bodies' is exemplified in 'Site of memory and dismemory: the Valley of the Fallen in Spain'. Its author, Andrea Hepworth, studies the Valle de los Caidos as a 'monumental memorial' conceived by and under Francisco Franco, and its 'dissonant heritage', a space with blurred distinctions between a monument, a mass grave and an unacknowledged site of suffering for political prisoners during its construction. The article further details the background of the memorial's construction, its silenced narratives and its contested place in contemporary Spain, underscored by the impact of Paul Preston's *The Spanish holocaust*.

Memory politics and dismemory also preoccupy Michelle Kelso and Daina Eglitis in 'Holocaust commemoration in Romania: Roma and the contested politics of memory and memorialization'. Kelso is a long-time activist for Roma, and the article reflects her and Eglitis's pursuit of a recognized presence for Roma in Romania's Holocaust memorial that was unveiled in Bucharest in 2009. The authors explore the emergence of hegemonic narratives in post-communist societies from a sociological perspective of power and social relations, suggesting that capital, and the power that it confers, 'are not equitably distributed in society'. They trace the history and experience of Romanian Roma during the Holocaust and their mis/representation and spatial marginalization in the Bucharest memorial.

The 1981 massacre of 1,000 men, women and children at El Mozote, a small town in northern Morazán, El Salvador, occurred at the beginning of the Salvadoran civil war. Rafael Alarcón Medina and Leigh Binford bring anthropological expertise to the study of the massacre's contested memory in 'Revisiting the El Mozote massacre: memory and politics in postwar El Salvador'. They explore the massacre's impact on the local history of the town, as a potential beneficiary of this dark history in relation to reparations, tourism and economic development, and critically assess the competing political interests that have directed narratives of the massacre.

The special issue, bringing together historians, anthropologists and sociologists, advances the study of genocide, violence and memory tourism as a vibrant interdisciplinary field. I thank the authors—recently graduated PhDs, mid-career scholars and senior professors—for their commitment and professionalism in dealing with revisions. I am also most grateful to the many anonymous reviewers who provided timely and rigorous feedback to authors, and to my co-editors, in particular, for supporting the idea of the workshop and for guiding its outcome as this special issue.

Thinking comparatively about genocide memorialization

REBECCA JINKS

This article argues for a comparative approach to studying genocide memorialization. Memorials and museums form an intrinsic part of state and society in post-conflict societies, and a comparative approach can capture the dynamics of memory politics and state building at play, especially the reception and instrumentalization in different national arenas of transitional justice mechanisms and the ways in which international agendas interact with domestic ones. The article first reviews the small existing comparative literature, and then offers a discussion of three potential comparative approaches: the transfer of representational strategies and discourses of remembrance by museum or memorial staff who serve as consultants for new projects; how genocide museums construct evidence or proof of genocide, and how these constructions might be received by victim and perpetrator groups in post-genocide societies, and by international visitors; and, finally, how the differences between official memorials and other places of memory might resist hegemonic state narratives.

Introduction

The study of memorials to genocide and other atrocities is now firmly entrenched as a field of inquiry. Many of these studies are richly nuanced, offering insights into the contexts and debates surrounding national and local memorials, memorials designed by 'starchitects' (Daniel Libeskind, for example) and others put together more spontaneously, memorials whose political lives spanned successive regimes and others that were never built. Whether studies of the German 'counter-monuments' of the 1960s onwards, the Rwandan government's selective remembering and preference for the macabre at its six national genocide memorials, or the campaigns of the Women of Srebrenica,[1] they point towards the ways in which states use the genocidal past in support of a particular national narrative, the multiple ways that societies engage or disengage with public commemorations, and indeed the growth in memorialization itself. These studies indicate broadly similar dynamics at play, notwithstanding the specificities of the national or local context; yet, to date, very few studies compare genocide memorialization. In this article, I make a case for the addition of the comparative method to the study of genocide memorialization. Just as comparative analysis in the fields of history and political science has enhanced our understanding of the specificities and parallels in the genocidal process, so too can a comparative approach to genocide memorialization illuminate how contexts and power relations shape remembrance and representation, and how meanings are made from the events in their aftermath. If genocide involves the violent destruction of community, then we might ask how the fact of genocide, or its denial, is used by political elites and ordinary people in different contexts to construct, or reconstruct, community in the aftermath. How has genocide been used for political and social purposes in different contexts? What influence has the international community had in these different aftermaths? Where have potentials for a different kind of civic society opened up, and where have they been closed down? What of cases not widely recognized as genocide, either domestically or globally?

The opening section discusses the few existing comparative studies, using them as a starting point for a consideration of how the comparative method might be applied to genocide memorialization—asking what it might add to our understanding of the processes and politics of memorialization beyond simply identifying ‘trends’, how it might negotiate the stark differences between cases, and whether it runs the risk of replicating debates from the historical arena. In part, the aim here is to suggest different thematic approaches and empirical openings that might expand the repertoire of this emerging field: to this end, the rest of the article identifies and explores some potentially useful points of comparison in the case studies on which my own research has focused—memorials and museums that commemorate genocide in Armenia, Cambodia, the Holocaust, the former Yugoslavia and Rwanda—and, where possible, to point towards other examples that might confirm or complicate these comparisons. In particular, I explore the diffusion of representational strategies and concepts across the global landscape of memorialization via the exchange of visits and expertise; how genocide museums construct evidence or proof of genocide, and how these constructions might be received by victim and perpetrator groups in post-genocide societies, and by international visitors; and how hegemonic state narratives might be disrupted by the differences between official memorials and local, often personal, memories and experiences of place and event.

Outlining the field

The Holocaust has, overwhelmingly, received the most attention in studies of genocide memorialization, although in the past decade or so the literature on other case studies has begun to grow (albeit unevenly; there are relatively few studies of Armenian memorialization, for example, whereas work on Cambodia and Rwanda is developing more strongly).[2] A substantial proportion of these publications focus on a single museum, memorial or ritual of public remembrance, although others look at the shape of national remembrance in both national and ‘local’ genocide memorials,[3] or compare the memorialization of one genocide in different national settings (e.g. James Young’s canonical work *The texture of memory* (1993)).[4] These studies are invaluable, because their analysis is often culturally sensitive and sophisticated in its application; the challenge with comparative research is to preserve these nuances and use them to build a picture of how a variety of actors, state or otherwise, negotiate shifting narratives about the past, cultural traditions of burial and mourning, and the realities of the aftermath in the pursuit of their own agendas.

Efforts at this kind of comparative research come, of course, with many attendant difficulties—not least the more prosaic issue of funding. But conceptually, too, comparative research requires careful setting up. Comparative historiography in the arenas of history, political science and anthropology has demonstrated the problems with taking one case study as a model or template—most frequently this has been the Holocaust—or with privileging similarities over differences in the search for a neat overarching explanation. This latter point is all the more pertinent when, as comparative work on memorialization would demand, one is attempting cross-cultural comparisons, where the nuances of each culture (including one's own) need to be acknowledged and preserved within the text. Alongside these is the issue of definition and inclusion that has often plagued comparative genocide studies, but where it seems that an inclusive but rigorous approach proves most productive. But lest this seem too daunting, it is worth noting that at the same time the comparative historiography has not only demonstrated that careful comparisons along these lines bring richer understandings, but has also made a strong argument for comparative work as a mechanism for defusing and diluting narratives of national or group exceptionalism, or what A. Dirk Moses has termed the 'phallic logic' of claims that 'my trauma is bigger than yours'—logics that are themselves so often involved in the genesis of genocide.[5] These are the challenges but also the impetus for studying genocide memorialization comparatively.

The two studies that have already taken up this challenge—Paul Williams' *Memorial museums* (2007) and Louis Bickford and Amy Sodaro's chapter in *Remembering for the future* (2010)[6]—discuss the museums and memorials as part of a 'global rush to commemorate atrocities' (Williams), or the 'internationalization of a new commemorative paradigm' (Bickford and Sodaro). Neither explicitly theorizes their comparative approach, and neither is restricted only to genocide memorialization, but both usefully discuss various global trends in these memorial museums: the encouragement of identification with the victims through displays of personal objects and individual or family photographs; the concern to allow visitors to 'experience' the site as an authentic space; and the underlying philosophy or goal of many of these institutions of creating a human rights culture and facilitating learning about the past in order to prevent genocide and violence in the future—trends that are neatly encapsulated by Bickford and Sodaro under the headings of 'empathy', 'experience' and 'education'. Quite rightly, both pieces criticize this underlying premise that sympathy for the victims and 'learning from the past' will somehow prevent violence in the future (indeed, learning *what* is always only vaguely conceptualized in such discourses, or translated into universal concepts such as learning 'tolerance', which hardly go to the root of the problem). Both works, then, offer wide-ranging analyses of the patterns of display in a wide variety of memorial museums, and the ways in which these museums have taken up and interpreted human rights discourses. In their analyses of these museums and memorials as manifestations of (or at least guided by) a human rights culture, though, both leave plenty more to be said about how and why human rights discourses were adopted (and by whom) in each case, what this might mean for shifting power relations, and whether they signify reform or merely lip-service. Williams does include a chapter on contestations over memory in the aftermath, but Bickford and Sodaro, who approach their examples primarily as being 'part of the transitional justice "tool kit"', do not have space in their short chapter to consider the social conflicts and rather less cosmopolitan and progressive narratives behind the establishment of many of these museums.[7]

A third example here is Jenny Edkins' *Trauma and the memory of politics* (2000/2003), which goes further in linking local or national politics behind memorialization with global trends. Her case studies, too, are not limited to genocide and are generally western—for example, the Irish famine, the Holocaust, WWI, and America's memory of Vietnam—but she combines quite lengthy analyses of certain of the individual memorials with her broader conclusions that, for example, the narratives at these memorials 'seem unable to get away from the rhetorics of state or nation, and they fail to escape the racialization upon which the genocides, enslavements and famines were themselves based' and also that, since roughly the 1990s and the emergence of globalized humanitarian power, a new narrative has come into force—one of rescue.[8] Edkins' nuanced analysis, which oscillates effectively between each case study and her broader argument, is a useful model for the kind of comparative work under consideration here.

In addition to these studies, there is also a growing literature on 'dark tourism' that seeks to chart and explain the seemingly increasing public interest in visiting sights and sites that can be labelled as 'dark', from the London Dungeons to Auschwitz.[9] Little real work has been conducted on genocide tourism itself thus far,[10] though, and at present much of the literature (which is rooted in the methodology of tourism studies) is concerned with typologizing the field into different categories of tourist sites, and indeed different shades of 'dark',[11] and discussing issues of supply and demand, 'visitor motivation' and 'morality'. This somewhat externalizing perspective has left largely open, however, questions of the content and messages of these 'dark' memorials and museums, the prior interpretations and understandings visitors bring with them to these sites, the social conflicts underlying memorialization, or indeed other sites that do not feature on the tourist trail but may be full of meaning for locals. Others—mostly anthropologists—have engaged with them, however, giving a rich insight into the 'touristic ways of seeing' (Paolo Favero) or 'touristic phantasms' (Victor Alneng)[12]—the prior conceptions, ideas, images and knowledge that mediate and often determine tourists' experience of place. In this vein, Rachel Hughes has discussed tourism in Cambodia under the rubric of 'dutiful tourism', showing how tourists' experiences of Tuol Sleng are often embedded within and guided by discourses of morality and humanitarianism, as well as the cultural imaginaries of the genocide and of Cambodia as an exotic and dangerous place: moral tourism and donations of everything from clothes to blood are conceived as an alternative to war tourism or sex tourism, and 'the shuttling from a tourist subjectivity to that of a humanitarian actor is common among travellers in Cambodia'.[13] Her interviews show that the Holocaust lingers in the back of western visitors' minds as an interpretive device and a model for 'moral witnessing', and that, in the absence of much historical narrative in the Tuol Sleng museum (which visitors seek in order to gain 'authoritative knowledge' about the past), many visitors reconceptualize their visit in terms of a symbolic gesture, 'no longer *epistemological* but *testimonial*, not "I now know more" but "I visited"'.[14] This kind of approach to tourism is useful because it engages seriously with the imaginaries—the 'ways of seeing' and the 'phantasms'—with which visitors arrive at these sites, and, crucially, how they negotiate with and interpret what they find at these museums, within those imaginaries and humanitarian and moral discourses.

This nascent literature offers promising ways of thinking comparatively about westerners' encounters with and interpretations of these genocide museums and memorials, particularly from the point of view of the shared cultural familiarity with both Holocaust memorialization and discourses of human rights. But they also point to certain lacunae, namely any properly comparative exploration of how memory politics operate in different societies in the aftermath of genocide at a national and local level. There is plenty of potential to build upon the depth and sophistication of specialists' writings here, and thereby to gain a different perspective on the uses of and responses to genocide in the aftermath, and how these memory interventions shape remembrance, community and interpretation in the aftermath of genocide. The challenge with this sort of undertaking will be to go beyond simply identifying trends or parallels—such as the display of horror to achieve political legitimacy for successor states in (for example) Rwanda and Cambodia,[15] the individualization of victims to encourage identification and empathy, the use of a particular style of interior design and architecture to create affect in purpose-built museums, or indeed the very fact of this widespread and official memorialization—and instead to look more deeply at what these trends and parallels might signify about how (and which) meanings are made in individual and global communities in the aftermath of genocide. Equally, a fair amount of agility will be called for in remaining sensitive to the national and local—not only of politics and society in the aftermath, but also how memorials and museums negotiate with (or disregard) the traditional rites and symbolisms of death, burial and remembrance, or the place and function museums occupy in different cultures[16]—while also considering the global. As Sharon Macdonald argues in *Difficult heritage* (2009), her excellent study of the memorialization at the Nuremberg Rally Grounds, memorialization is never culturally isolated:

> Rather, the local is negotiated into being in relation—sometimes through cultural analogy, sometimes via shared concepts and practices, sometimes through the intervention of factors from outside, and sometimes through explicit opposition—to 'elsewhere', be that other cities nearby or other parts of the world. ... Furthermore, not only are local actions refracted through concepts and debates from elsewhere, they are often undertaken in awareness of a potential international—and judgemental—gaze, whether that of tourists or politicians.[17]

This, then, has the potential to be an open, creative and interdisciplinary field of study, one that might tackle the intellectual and philosophical question of *how* genocide can be represented (a question that has largely only been asked of the Holocaust thus far)[18] as well as questions of state violence and nation building in the aftermath of genocide, the nature of diasporic remembrance, or responses to memorialization by post-genocide communities and international visitors. Below I offer three brief examples of potentially interesting lines of enquiry: firstly, the cross-fertilization of ideas and representational strategies across memorial contexts and cases; secondly, constructions of evidence in memorialization; and thirdly, the possible limits of hegemonic state memorial narratives. These brief outlines are not intended as fully worked-through pieces of research, or a proposal (of sorts) for a somehow comprehensive, comparative project. Rather, I hope to signal, in the vein of my comments above, some of the different ways in which comparative research into genocide memorialization might offer new or deeper ways of thinking about the politics of memory in the aftermath.

Institutional interconnections

One very concrete way of tracing the 'globalization' of memory cultures, particularly the diffusion of human rights discourses and norms and memorial strategies, is to conduct in-depth institutional histories of the design and development of memorials and museums. Here the question of when, why and how post-genocide states and institutions take up the language of transitional justice mechanisms—the language of truth, reconciliation, forgiveness and prevention through education and commemoration—can be examined. A comparative perspective would then be able to offer an understanding of how human rights norms have spread—or, in a less passive construction, have been instrumentalized by post-conflict states with their own agendas—and whether this might signal deep societal change or, rather, be an indication of both the ubiquity and lack of influence of the international community's human rights agenda. Within this scope, one particular approach would be to focus on the direct transfer of ideas, approaches and strategies from one case to another, via the sharing of institutional expertise or the use of one or more museums as inspiration for a new project.

A very clear example of established institutions acting as consultants for the development of a new museum is that of the UK charity Aegis Trust's involvement in Rwandan memorialization.[19] The founders of Aegis, Steven and James Smith, run Beth Shalom Holocaust Centre, an educational centre in Nottinghamshire established in 1995, itself partly inspired by a visit to Yad Vashem in 1991. The mayor of Kigali and officials in the Ministry of Culture were seeking to establish a national memorial in time for the 2004 anniversary commemorations of the genocide, and travelled to Yad Vashem and several European Holocaust sites, which they determined too large and expensive as templates for Kigali; at Beth Shalom they found 'a better approximation of what they were looking for', writes Amy Sodaro.[20] Aegis took over responsibility for raising money for the museum and education centre, and the centre's operation (Kigali donated the land and agreed to maintain the building); the funding target was reached just four months before the anniversary. The Smiths and a team of 50 Rwandans drafted the exhibition narrative and panels, with minimal intervention from Rwandan officials, according to James Smith, and their plan for the site was 'modelled on' their own experience at Beth Shalom.[21] Aegis has since also been involved in developing the new museum at Murambi, which opened in 2011.

The permanent exhibition at Kigali has three sections: the first, Wasted Lives, explores genocides around the world, placing Rwanda in context; the second and largest, Genocide, tells the story of the Rwandan genocide; the third is a memorial exhibition dedicated to the child victims.[22] The museum (and the Murambi exhibition), in design and layout, is very reminiscent of the general style that has been used for Holocaust museums and permanent exhibits in the past three decades: dark colour palettes, the use of architecture and space to elicit certain emotions in visitors (looming walls, physical descents at key narrative moments, disorienting paths), and the use of survivor testimony, individualizing photographs of the victims and a wall of names, each of which helps to communicate the human scale of the tragedy. The narrative of the exhibitions, in line with the government's state-building agenda, emphasizes the essential indivisibility of the nation: Hutu and Tutsi lived together peaceably before the colonists divided society along ethnic lines, and post-independence elites incited successive waves of violence against the Tutsi, which culminated in genocide; 'the nation', freed from this tyranny, can now mourn its victims. Noticeably, though, the conclusion of this narrative of a nation coming together once again is suffused with the international language of transitional justice mechanisms—reconciliation, peace, forgiveness, healing, remembrance. As Rachel Ibreck notes, here we can perceive transnational practices of memorialization, and the fusion of local imperatives and imaginaries with international norms.[23]

Not dissimilarly, staff from the Memorial Centre at Westerbork, a Nazi transit camp in Holland, and Suzanne Bardgett, then curator of the Holocaust exhibition and the Crimes Against Humanity exhibition at London's Imperial War Museum, both shared their expertise with the staff and survivors setting up the Potočari Memorial Centre in the battery factory just outside Srebrenica. Dirk Mulder, director of Westerbork, was firm that 'Westerbork can and will not provide a blueprint of how the Potočari Memorial Centre can look like [sic]', but gave plenty of help, information and sharing of experience and expertise.[24] Between 2001 and 2005 reciprocal visits for staff were organized, training was given to the Bosnian staff and some technical equipment was lent to Potočari. Mulder noted in particular that Westerbork's project 'A Name and a Face', which concentrates on individuals' stories in order to humanize the victims and guide remembrance and education, might be useful for Srebrenica. At the Potočari Memorial Centre today, two huge black cubes have been constructed inside the former battery factory. One houses a display of the photographs and biographies of fifteen of the roughly 8,000 murdered Muslim men and boys, together with a small personal object exhumed from the mass grave. Suzanne Bardgett was involved in designing the exhibition at this stage: 'We chose twenty artefacts ... to represent the kinds of personal effects that were being excavated: a key, a pair of spectacles, a handkerchief, a copy of the Koran—each providing evidence of genocidal murder but also offering a link back to life in the Srebrenica enclave'.[25] The other cube is used for screening an adaptation of British director Leslie Woodhead's 1999 documentary, *A cry from the grave*, which includes harrowing testimony from the mothers, sisters and wives who survived Srebrenica. Bardgett, too, expressed the international concern for reconciliation: 'Whatever kind of memorial room was built would have to do justice to this appalling tragedy, but the need for society to rebuild had to be borne in mind too. The Memorial Room should be a place to mourn and to remember, rather than to provoke and accuse'.[26]

Both of these examples bring up the question of how far Holocaust memorialization is the paradigm, or template, that is being transferred.[27] At this point it is necessary to disaggregate 'the Holocaust': certainly, quite clearly, one sees the transfer of *representational strategies* that are currently most prominent in Holocaust memorialization to other contexts—in particular the dark, oppressing, dimly lit interior design now common to most purpose-built Holocaust museums, and the attempt to create empathy for and identification with the victims via individual stories, family photographs and lists of victims' names—although it is important to note that these strategies are symptomatic of much broader shifts in western cultural institutions and culture, and were never only associated with this trend in Holocaust memorialization. One also sees, as detailed above, the transfer of *discourses* and *norms* of remembrance, which emphasize the Holocaust injunction of 'never again' and education for prevention, as well as the broader transitional justice language of truth, justice and forgiveness. But what is crucial here, lest this merely confirm the thesis of a global cosmopolitan memory largely derived from the Holocaust,[28] is to look through and beyond these discourses to ask whether the universalism inherent in them is truly meant, or whether empathy for the victims and a hasty push for reconciliation might conceal old and new injustices in the present, or be part of a geopolitical strategy that aims to portray to international powers and funders the image of a former 'failed state' en route to democratization and modernization.[29]

Evidence in memorialization

The discourses surrounding 'evidence' in relation to genocide memorialization are a second potentially fruitful area of research, since they often go to the heart of conflicts over the narration and *meaning* of the past in post-genocide societies. My interest here is less in the narratives of the 'truth' of genocide themselves, than in what kinds of evidence are marshalled in their service. In Rwanda and Cambodia, the rows of skulls and bones on display are often invoked as evidence by political elites; in the Armenian Genocide Museum, alongside the infamous Talaat telegrams, the cabinets are full of foreign eyewitness reports; in Bosnia, the use of forensic analysis and DNA testing to identify the dead has lent a slightly different air to the construction of and discourses around evidence, although the

Potočari Memorial Centre itself places more emphasis on survivor testimony and personal objects exhumed along with the dead as evidence.

These artefacts and objects are often straightforwardly (and repeatedly) invoked as evidence, especially in Rwanda and Cambodia[30]—but, as Hughes writes, these claims demand further attention.[31] While at one level the displays of human remains, atrocity photographs and indeed the physical spread of the cemeteries in Srebrenica or Sarajevo may conform with the western tourist's basic conception of genocide as 'mass death', these artefacts are not usually in and of themselves sufficient *legal* evidence to prove genocide—specifically, its intent.[32] One can even question the need for this (emphasis on) evidence—as Hughes points out, '[g]iven that the Democratic Kampuchea period significantly affected all sectors of Cambodian society, there seems little need to have prioritized such evidence for a population who had had proof enough already: that is, the survivors who had themselves been materially and psychologically affected'.[33] The point here is that while the claims appear straightforward, the way these artefacts are made to work in post-genocide societies is not: the choice of some types of evidence over others is deliberate, and very often what underlies this choice is a contestation over the *meaning* of a mass death.

In Rwanda, for example, the government insists (since 2008) upon the genocide as a genocide of the Tutsi; the identity officially imparted onto these bones is therefore Tutsi, since to say in Rwanda that Hutu also died opens one up to accusation and persecution as a purveyor of the 'double genocide theory'.[34] Yet, as Guyer notes, 'anybody can make bones', and some Rwandans may suspect, or may *know*, that Hutu bones are also on display—whether murdered because of their opposition to the genocide, or by the Rwandan Patriotic Front (RPF) as part of retaliation campaigns.[35] To insist upon these bones as evidence for a specifically Tutsi genocide, therefore, is a raw display of power over Hutu mourning their own relatives, and further entrenches the divisions between Hutu and Tutsi in post-genocide Rwanda.[36] It also rides roughshod over more 'traditional' burial rites in Rwandan culture, where Rwandans try, as far as possible, to maintain a link with the dead by burying them around their homes, not in cemeteries, and where the display of human remains is thought to conjure the deceased's ghost (*umuzimu*) in a manner that may be dangerous.[37] As Meierhenrich has argued, the government's refusal to allow the burial of these bones 'seems to have served, more often than not, the purpose of legitimating authoritarian rule rather than honoring the genocide dead'—by pursuing a 'strategy of suffering' vis-à-vis the international community, and also, as Guyer argues, justifying a repressive government 'by presenting a spectre of past violence as a permanent future possibility'.[38] This final point could also be observed of Cambodia, where, as Judy Ledgerwood wrote in 1997, 'the central message of the government was, and remains to this day: you must support us because to fail to do so will result in the return to power of the Khmer Rouge'.[39] Although Prime Minister Hun Sen signalled the end of the Khmer Rouge as a political danger in 1998 when he encouraged Cambodians to 'dig a hole and bury the past',[40] one can argue that these memorials still serve as a legitimation of the Hun Sen government (as David Chandler notes, with continuing tourism to these sites and the current trial of Khmer Rouge leaders, 'the hole into which the past is to be buried, in other words, has only been partially dug or partially filled in').[41] Here, too, the display of human remains runs counter to Cambodian rituals surrounding death, in which the dead are cremated; the malevolent ghosts of those who died violent or unnatural deaths are thought to haunt the place in which they died.[42] One common rationale given for the (continued) display of the skulls in Cambodia is the education of future generations,[43] but that does not explain why it has to be this particular *form* of evidence. While this rationale might seem to be supported by Burcu Münyas's finding that Cambodian youth in fact often do not believe their parents' stories about the Khmer Rouge, the main thrust of her article would suggest that this has more to do with the lack of education about Cambodia's recent past than the power of the bones of the dead.[44]

The workings of evidence in Armenia are very different. What is interesting about the Armenian Genocide Museum in its current configuration (at the time of writing, the original 1995 exhibition is being revised and expanded for the centenary commemorations in 2015) is that there is almost no survivor testimony: a couple of the display cases contain books and diaries by Armenian survivors, but one can only see their covers or the two open pages dictated by the museum, whereas other display cases are bursting with reports, diaries, newspapers and testimonies written by foreign observers. In part this is a continuation of other Armenian acts of memory, which have seen Yerevan streets renamed after foreigners who helped the Armenians, and earth from their graves buried at Tsitsernakaberd, which Tsypylma Darieva describes as a conversion of 'an ethnic notion of loss and death into a global memory of forgotten human loss'.[45] But if one reconsiders the exhibition content from an evidentiary point of view—its main aim is to make the case for genocide—then, alongside the 'smoking gun' of the Young Turks' orders and the large-scale reproductions of atrocity photographs (mostly taken by German soldier Armin Wegner), one wonders whether emphasis is placed on *foreign* testimony because it may be seen as more 'reliable', particularly by the visiting dignitaries and tourists whom the museum is hoping to persuade. Evidence here is deliberately aimed at convincing the international community of genocide and, perhaps, creating an obligation to recognize it *as* genocide.[46]

The discourses surrounding evidence in Bosnia, and at Srebrenica particularly, are also indicative of the importance of the international community. Sarah E. Wagner's insightful analysis of the use of DNA testing and forensic analysis to identify the Srebrenica missing shows how these technological innovations have affected notions of evidence and 'proof' among both the international community and survivors, tending to satisfy the former's preference for impartiality and scientific evidence, while interacting in far more subtle ways with the latter's individual memories of the events.[47] Some references to the forensic exhumations appear at the Potočari Memorial Centre itself, along with some choice quotes from Radovan Karadžić, Ratko Mladić and others, and a copy of the Hague's February 2007 verdict of genocide, but just as important in terms of 'evidence' here, in my opinion, are the personal objects and short biographies on display in the exhibition, and the emphasis on testimony from the female survivors in the Memorial Centre's film. This evidence speaks to personal or communal memory and the mourning process, rather than evidence as legitimizing state power or a case for genocide.

A few things can be observed from these four cases. While there is always a selection process when museum and memorial displays are being designed, one can see that in some cases, particular artefacts are chosen for display (and explicitly invoked as evidence) in a way that dovetails with other state goals and policies. On an interconnected point, taking a comparative perspective highlights a great variance in how oral or survivor testimony is used in different cases—from its prevalence in Holocaust commemoration in the last few decades, to the dearth in the Armenian Genocide Museum, or indeed its contestation by conservative commentators in Australia as a reliable source of information about the Aboriginal experience of settler colonialism.[48] In part this has to do, rather unfairly, with the disputation of cases *as* genocide, but further work would also need to locate attitudes towards testimony in their proper socio-cultural moment (for example, Holocaust testimony and survivors have not always been revered in quite the same way).[49] Finally, evidence often also works differently among national or local communities and the international community; for example, the forensic evidence gathered at Srebrenica, and indeed the arguments of the International Criminal Tribunal for the former Yugoslavia (ICTY) prosecution lawyers, made little difference to Serbian public opinion, but the public broadcasting of a video of Serbian police forces executing a group of young Muslim men following the Srebrenica massacre in 1995 had a singular effect in changing perceptions.[50]

Disrupting hegemonic narratives

One of the most pertinent areas for research into the aftermath of genocide is the question of how the fact of genocide—or its denial—is used in the rebuilding (or re-envisioning) of society and community afterwards. I mean to encapsulate here a wide range of examples and processes, including the ways in which the new Turkish state's silence over or denial of the persecution of its minorities aided (and still aids) its nation-building project; the Rwandan state's double-discourse, which bans the categories of 'Hutu' and 'Tutsi' at the official and public level, but continues to operate in ways that reinforce those categories at a more subtle level;[51] and the various practices that create and maintain a Srebrenica community, even as its members may be physically dispersed—communal burials at the Potočari Memorial Centre, activism and campaigns (led by the Women of Srebrenica), and informal group meetings of survivors that provide support.[52] Memorialization is one arena in which competing (and occasionally overlapping) actors and interest groups—from the state to civic activist groups, local communities and private individuals—stake their claims to speak on behalf of the dead, as part of their claim for legitimacy in shaping the future. As I suggested above, memorialization can be seen as an *intervention* into memory (and thus the present), since memorialization tends to involve decisive statements about *what* should be remembered (and what 'forgotten'), who the victims were (and were not) and on whose behalf they are remembered (the nation, a local community, 'humanity')—and in this sense they often tend, and intend, to be normative.

There are plenty of angles to take within this rubric, including asking which memorial initiatives set themselves up to be hegemonic (i.e. state commemorations, national museums and memorials), and which speak locally, oppositionally or privately;[53] how traditional rites of burial and commemoration are co-opted into memorialization, and how far they might give a sense of continuity and 'restored' community (and, linked, how accompanying religious discourses interpret and bestow meaning); what more spontaneous forms of commemoration arise in the immediate aftermath, and whether any become formalized into official or widespread commemorative practices (e.g. the *yizker bikher* written in the displaced persons camps after 1945 and onwards,[54] or the Women of Srebrenica's collection of photographs of the missing donated from surviving family members, which are intended to one day form part of the display in the Potočari Memorial Centre[55]). One might also think about memorialization in former perpetrator societies, including silences, direct denial or facing up to violent pasts, how group or national identity is negotiated in the aftermath, and how these discourses develop or endure over time. But another avenue, which I want to explore in a little more depth here, is that of the extent to which the state tries, and is successful, in exerting control over local memorialization—or the extent to which official memorialization can succeed in being hegemonic.

Of the current research that compares national with local museums and memorials, most finds that the state's hand means there are significant convergences in form and narrative. Hughes notes that local memorials in Cambodia were built according to a government decree of 1983, and are almost all in the form of a *stupa* filled with uncremated human remains, in much the same style of the Choeung Ek stupa (built later, in 1988);[56] Meierhenrich quite rightly notes that not all Rwandan memorials involve the display of human remains, or in quite the same way as the six national genocide memorials, but nevertheless the theme of heavy state control over the production of memorial space runs through his analysis;[57] the local memorials in Armenia built during the Soviet period (after public demonstrations in 1965, on the fiftieth anniversary of the genocide, petitioned the Party to allow commemoration) all conform to the Soviet socialist-realist style.[58] There are often small design differences at the local level, a result of different groups coming together to design and create these memorials, but these differences tend to be less significant than the overall similarities. Certainly this tells us something about states' desire for control, but I also believe it is important to put these local memorials into their lived context, and ask what place these memorials occupy in everyday life. Meierhenrich makes an important distinction between 'memorials' and 'loci' in Rwanda—the first being products of 'intentional design' which 'result from an *intentional encoding* of place' and the second being imbued with memory as part of a 'spontaneous encoding of place'[59]—which is useful to think with here. Might some memorials not also be loci? And thus how might the strength of individual or shared memory, imbued in these spaces *as* loci, disrupt hegemonic state memorial narratives? How might this change over time (with changing social and political contexts, with the waning of memory and with new generations)?

Here, the place of these memorials in public life can also be important. Some stupa in Cambodia, and some churches in Rwanda which now house the bones of the dead, presumably only really play a part in public life once a year, during national commemoration ceremonies. But there are others which, by dint of location or lack of funding for new municipal buildings, are part of everyday life as both civic spaces and loci. The church at Kibeho in Rwanda, for example, has been partitioned into a church with an ossuary and memorial at the back; many local memorials in Cambodia are within the grounds of restored wats. We might then ask how the annual state memorial narratives are received by local populations for whom these memorials are also loci; we can also ask that question more generally. As I noted above, for example, there is significant disagreement among ordinary Rwandans with the state's policy of displaying human remains at national memorials, and of refusing to allow Rwandans to bury the identified remains of their relatives at home.[60] But the state narrative of remembrance for the Tutsi dead at these memorials will also not chime for those Hutu whose relatives were killed during the genocide. And while Judy Ledgerwood found (in 1997) that most Khmer accepted the state narrative at Tuol Sleng—and thus perhaps also at local memorials, particularly during state-led commemorations—as largely true to their experiences,[61] Münyas's research into Cambodian youths' knowledge of the Khmer Rouge era suggests different encodings of these places by younger generations.[62]

Here the issue of change over time also becomes relevant. In Armenia, too, ordinary people's interpretations of the central memorial have changed in response to social and political developments. As Darieva notes, over the lifetime of the memorial obelisk at Tsitsernakaberd—which is riven by a vertical split into a taller, larger part and a smaller, thinner one—the Armenian population has variously seen the larger part as symbolizing Russia and the smaller the Republic of Armenia, or ancient Armenia and its present-day territory, or, during the Karabakh conflict, the larger Armenia and the smaller the self-proclaimed Ngorno-Karabakh conflict.[63] Similar points can be made about various sites of Holocaust remembrance that have seen a succession of socio-political changes, each of which has imbued them with new 'official' meanings—and which have sometimes been modified as a result. Auschwitz is a prime example of a site of memory remade in the image of current politics,[64] but what of the more local sites of memory—a ruined synagogue, a wall made of Jewish tombstones—which, largely ignored throughout the Cold War years, have in recent years taken on new significance as Polish memories of the Holocaust shift from the communist anti-fascist narrative, to new narratives of Polish national suffering after 1989, and in recent years towards incorporating more cosmopolitan narratives of Polish-Jewish suffering? At these particular sites, this mix of Polish memories will also entangle with those of other (usually Jewish) visitors who have, in recent decades, begun to search out the traces of the Jewish past in contemporary Poland, adding further complexity to the mix of memories at each site.[65] And as Rachel Hughes' analysis of 'dutiful tourism' in Cambodia points out, tourists are complicating (and in some ways commercializing) the mix of memories at genocide memorials around the world.

There are, of course, different degrees (and means) by which states attempt to impose a hegemonic memory of genocide. But in the end, hegemonic state narratives may not be normative; or, to borrow from Stuart Hall's famous formulation,[66] the issue is not only one of states encoding, but also of publics *decoding*. The study of memories at local genocide memorials can show how the vagaries of lived experience, the lapse of time, generational differences and the presence of tourists can disrupt state narratives; comparative work can identify patterns across cases, but also identify how global trends and shifts impact these local memories—not just the seismic changes that the fall of communism brought, but the rise of the globalized humanitarian power Jenny Edkins identifies, and its links with new forms of tourism.

Conclusion

Comparative work on the memorialization of genocide would seem to be a field ripe for further consideration. Far from being a peripheral or merely 'cultural' activity, memorialization is an intrinsic part of the operation of state and society in the aftermath, and studying it provides alternative perspectives on memory, power and state building in traumatized and divided societies, particularly in a context where the international community is taking an increasing interest in 'post-conflict resolution' and genocide memorials are becoming a staple of international tourism. Comparative work such as that I have outlined above will help to capture the interconnections between these dynamics in post-genocide societies—not only to trace patterns of memory and representation in different cultural contexts, but hopefully also to explore and explain the broader transnational and global currents that shape local memorialization. Such research will illuminate the differences—and transferences—between the memorialization of genocide and the memorialization of war, terrorism and other tragedies, and will enrich our understanding more generally of the dynamics of power, memory and representation in the aftermath of genocide.

Endnotes

1 James E. Young, 'The counter-monument: memory against itself in Germany today', *Critical Inquiry*, Vol. 18, No. 2, 1992, pp. 267–296; Jens Meierhenrich, 'Topographies of remembering and forgetting', in Scott Straus and Lars Waldorf (eds.), *Remaking Rwanda: state building and human rights after mass violence* (Madison, WI: University of Wisconsin Press, 2011), pp. 283–296; Selma Leydesdorff, *Surviving the Bosnian genocide: the Women of Srebrenica speak* (Bloomington: Indiana University Press, 2011).

2 On Armenia: Tsypylma Darieva, '"The road to Golgotha": representing loss in postsocialist Armenia', *Focaal – European Journal of Anthropology*, Vol. 52, 2008, pp. 92–108; Darieva, 'From silenced to voiced: changing politics of memory of loss in Armenia', in Darieva and Wolfgang Kaschuba (eds.), *Representations on the margins of Europe: politics and identities in the Baltic and south Caucasian states* (Frankfurt: Campus Verlag, 2007), pp. 65–88; Rebecca Jinks, 'Situating Tsitsernakaberd: the Armenian Genocide Museum in a global context', *International Journal of Armenian Genocide Studies* (forthcoming). Rather than listing all of the studies on Cambodia and Rwanda here, I direct the reader to the endnotes below.

3 See especially Rachel Hughes, 'Memory and sovereignty in post-1979 Cambodia: Choeung Ek and local genocide memorials', in Susan E. Cook (ed.), *Genocide in Cambodia and Rwanda: new perspectives* (New Brunswick, NJ: Transaction, 2006), pp. 257–279, and Meierhenrich, 'Topographies of remembering and forgetting'.

4 James E. Young, *The texture of memory: Holocaust memorials and meaning* (New Haven: Yale University Press, 1993). This kind of study is almost entirely limited to the memorialization of the Holocaust, for the obvious reason that there is little memorialization of other genocides outside the countries in which they occurred. (Comparative) studies of diasporic memorialization would seem to be a productive line to follow, though, especially as regards the maintenance of identity; the Armenian case would seem to be the clearest-cut example, but one could also look at the Cambodian Cultural Museum and Killing Fields Memorial in Seattle (2004) and the Cambodian American Heritage Museum and Killing Fields Memorial, Chicago (2004). On Armenian diasporic memorialization, see Natasha Azarian, 'La commemoration du genocide arménien à Fresno en Californie et à Yerevan en Arménie', *Socio-Anthropologie*, Vol. 22, 2008, pp. 145–162 and *Memorials of sorrow, remembrance and struggle* (Yerevan: Ministry of Diaspora of the Republic of Armenia, 2010). There are two recent and insightful articles on Cambodian-American diasporic remembrance: Cathy J. Schlund-Vials, 'Cambodian American memory work: justice and the "Cambodian syndrome"', *Positions*, Vol. 20, No. 3, 2012, pp. 805–830 and Katharya Um, 'Exiled memory: history, identity, and remembering in southeast Asia and southeast Asian diaspora', *Positions*, Vol. 20, No. 3, 2012, pp. 831–850. Dirk Moses' recent article on the role of competitive identity politics of various diaspora communities in the making/designing of the Canadian Museum for Human Rights offers several productive avenues of thought: A. Dirk Moses, 'The Canadian Museum for Human Rights: the "uniqueness of the Holocaust" and the question of genocide', *Journal of Genocide Research*, Vol. 14, No. 2, 2012, pp. 215–238.

5 A. Dirk Moses, 'Empire, colony, genocide: keywords and the philosophy of history', in Moses (ed.), *Empire, colony, genocide: conquest, occupation, and subaltern resistance in world history* (New York: Berghahn Books, 2008), p. 6.

6 Paul Williams, *Memorial museums: the global rush to commemorate atrocities* (Oxford and New York: Berg, 2007); Louis Bickford and Amy Sodaro, 'Remembering yesterday to protect tomorrow: the internationalization of a new commemorative paradigm', in Yifat Gutman, Adam D. Brown and Amy Sodaro (eds.), *Memory and the future: transnational politics, ethics and society* (Basingstoke: Palgrave Macmillan, 2010), pp. 66–86. Terence M. Duffy has written what is ostensibly a survey article, 'Museums of "human suffering" and the struggle for human rights', *Museum International*, Vol. 53, No. 1, 2001, pp. 10–16, but it remains a superficial, uncritical and occasionally factually incorrect list.

7 Bickford and Sodaro, 'Remembering yesterday', p. 69. They do briefly discuss memorials as part of nation-building practices (pp. 70–72, esp. p. 71), but also argue that they contribute to the 'democratisation of memory' (pp. 72–76) through the remembrance of individuals. One concrete example of their glossing over of the less progressive narratives in these museums is that they note that the Museum of Genocide Victims in Vilnius also displays personal possessions in its reconstructed torture cells, for example, but do not mention the museum's competitive and distasteful minimizing of the Nazi occupiers' crimes in order to emphasize those of the two Soviet occupations (for an excellent (and comparative) discussion, see James Mark, 'Containing fascism: history in post-Communist Baltic occupation and genocide museums', in Péter Apor and Oksana Sarkisova (eds.), *Past for the eyes: East European representations of communism in cinema and museums after 1989* (Budapest and New York: Central European University Press, 2008), pp. 335–369). As well as this general minimizing of the social conflicts that these museums very often gloss over—a fact that in itself limits the effectiveness of the museums' strategies to create a culture of human rights—they do not include cases that are too contested for these 'transitional justice tools' to work, such as Armenia or Spain.

8 Jenny Edkins, *Trauma and the memory of politics* (Cambridge: Cambridge University Press, 2003[2000]), p. 171. Although most closely focused on Holocaust museums, Chapter 4, 'Concentration camp museums', is the chapter that comes closest to the kind of comparative work I am proposing here.

9 Much of the recent literature originates in the new Institute for Dark Tourism Research at the University of Central Lancashire, headed by Philip Stone and Richard Sharpley. Earlier publications include John Lennon and Malcom Foley's *Dark tourism: the attraction of death and disaster* (London: Continuum, 2000).

10 John Beech's chapter 'Genocide tourism', in Philip R. Stone and Richard Sharpley (eds.), *The darker side of travel: the theory and practice of dark tourism* (Bristol: Channel View Publications, 2009), pp. 207–223, is one of the only surveys of specifically genocide tourism. However, it manages to give a skewed definition of genocide despite consulting the UN Genocide Convention (pp. 207–209), spends far too much time listing the reasons for Turkish denial of the Armenian genocide (pp. 213–214) and writes of the 'Schwansee conference' (p. 211).

11 Philip R. Stone, 'A dark tourism spectrum: towards a typology of death and macabre related tourist sites, attractions and exhibitions', *Tourism*, Vol. 54, No. 2, 2006, pp. 145–160. Stone divides 'the dark tourism product' (p. 152) into 'seven dark suppliers': dark fun factories, dark exhibitions, dark dungeons, dark resting places, dark shrines, dark conflict sites and dark camps of genocide (pp. 152–157). Richard Sharpley's 'Shedding light on dark tourism: an introduction', in Stone and Sharpley, *The darker side of travel*, pp. 3–22, then tables a different typology (p. 11): Perilous Places (towns of horror, dangerous destinations); Houses of Horror (dungeons of death, heinous hotels); Fields of Fatality (bloody battlegrounds, the hell of the Holocaust, cemeteries for celebrities); Tours of Torment (mayhem and murder, the now notorious); and Themed Thanatos (morbid museums, monuments to morality). He also suggests a spectrum from 'pale tourism' through 'grey supply' and 'grey demand' to 'black tourism' (p. 20). As Rachel Hughes notes, 'Tourisms to sites of mass political violence are significantly more complex than current "dark tourism" or "(a)moral tourism" theories suggest, in large part because such theories generalize and diminish that which they purport to explain'. Hughes, 'Dutiful tourism: encountering the Cambodian genocide', *Asia Pacific Viewpoint*, Vol. 49, No. 3, 2008, pp. 327–328, 320.

12 See Victor Alneng's brilliant '"What the fuck is a Vietnam?": touristic phantasms and the popcolonization of (the) Vietnam (War)', *Critique of Anthropology*, Vol. 22, No. 4, 2002, pp. 461–489 and Paolo Favero's engaging '"What a wonderful world!": on the touristic ways of seeing, the knowledge and the politics of the "culture industries of otherness"', *Tourist Studies*, Vol. 7, No. 1, 2007, pp. 51–81; also Alneng, 'The modern does not cater for natives: travel ethnography and the conventions of form', *Tourist Studies*, Vol. 2, No. 2, 2002, pp. 119–142.

13 Hughes, 'Dutiful tourism', p. 327. I do wonder if Hughes is being a little hegemonic in her characterization of tourists to Cambodia, though—or rather, whether there might not also be some rapid shuttling of the tourist subjectivity from humanitarian actor at Tuol Sleng to warzone tourist (or indeed young, carefree and drunk backpacker) elsewhere in Phnom Penh. The most explicit version of this shuttling would be the bizarre day trip that most tuk tuk drivers will offer tourists—from Tuol Sleng to Choeung Ek, and then on to the shooting range further down the road, where bullets are $1 each, or one can bazooka a cow for $100. More generally, one could note the tourist tat capitalizing on the dangers of Cambodia's minefields—t-shirts and postcards declaring 'I survived Cambodia!'. See Tim Winters, 'When ancient glory meets modern tragedy: Angkor and the Khmer Rouge in contemporary tourism', in Leakthina Chau-Pech Ollier and Tim Winter (eds.), *Expressions of Cambodia: the politics of tradition, identity and change* (Abingdon: Routledge, 2006), pp. 37–53.

14 Hughes, 'Dutiful tourism', pp. 327, 326.

15 Meierhenrich, 'Topographies of remembering and forgetting', esp. p. 292; Judy Ledgerwood, 'The Cambodia Tuol Sleng Museum of Genocidal Crimes: national narrative', *Museum Anthropology*, Vol. 21, No. 1, 1997, pp. 82–98.

16 Ingrid Muan's 'Musings on museums from Phnom Penh', in Ivan Karp et al. (eds.), *Museum frictions: public cultures/global transformations* (Durham and London: Duke University Press, 2006), pp. 257–285, is an engaging discussion of the practices of museum-going in Cambodia, which are only awkwardly related to western practices but are, of course, still heavily involved in the production of meaning. Rwanda could be a good comparator in this respect, but there is no reason not to deconstruct western museum-going practices also (indeed, this is one way of furthering studies into 'dark tourism'). On non-western museums more generally, see Christina Kreps, 'Non-western models of museums and curation in cross-cultural perspective', in Sharon Macdonald (ed.), *A companion to museum studies* (Oxford: Blackwell, 2006), pp. 457–472.

17 Sharon Macdonald, *Difficult heritage: negotiating the Nazi past in Nuremberg and beyond* (Abingdon: Routledge, 2009), pp. 5, 7.

18 Sara Guyer has made some interesting comments in this regard about the display of skulls at Rwandan memorials: 'On the one hand, they commemorate genocide *as* genocide. That is, they commemorate the annihilation (or intended annihilation) of a population rather than persons, and thus they bear witness to the difference between genocide and death in general. The memorials—such as they are—cannot and do not memorialize individual deaths and proper names. Yet, by refusing to return names, identities, or individualities to the dead, they either recur to genocide's logic (which also is colonialism's logic)—that is, the logic of impersonality whereby persons are recognized only as members of a population—or they commemorate death-in-general, rather than the specific violence of genocide. … If to remember the dead as individuals (to restore names and faces)—in the name of recovered dignity and propriety—is to *fail* to remember the very specific violence that attends genocide as violence against a population, to remember the dead through the sheer anonymity of these bones means that no one is or can be remembered.' Guyer, 'Rwanda's bones', *boundary 2*, Vol. 36, No. 2, 2009, p. 163. Rachel Hughes has made some similar comments about Choeung Ek's memorial stupa in Phnom Penh, marshalling Agamben's concept of 'bare life': Hughes, 'Fielding genocide: post-1979 Cambodia and the geopolitics of memory' (PhD thesis, University of Melbourne, 2006),

p. 99. See also Marc Nichanian, *The historiographic perversion*, trans. Gil Anidjar (New York: Colombia University Press, 2009), especially Chapter 4, 'Testimony: from document to monument'.

19 See Amy Sodaro, 'Politics of the past: remembering the Rwandan genocide at the Kigali Memorial Centre', in Erica Lehrer, Cynthia E. Milton and Monica Eileen Patterson (eds.), *Curating difficult knowledge: violent pasts in public places* (Basingstoke: Palgrave Macmillan, 2011), pp. 72–89. See also Rachel Ibreck, 'International constructions of national memories: the aims and effects of foreign donors' support for genocide remembrance in Rwanda', *Journal of Intervention and Statebuilding*, Vol. 7, No. 2, 2013, p. 158.

20 Sodaro, 'Politics of the past', p. 78.

21 Ibreck, 'International constructions', p. 159.

22 See Sodaro, 'Politics of the past', pp. 79–83, for an extended analytic description of the Kigali exhibition.

23 Ibreck, 'International constructions', p. 159.

24 See Dirk Mulder, 'International experiences on commemoration of war atrocities', unpublished conference presentation, Sarajevo, 12 July 2005.

25 Suzanne Bardgett, 'Remembering Srebrenica', *History Today*, Vol. 57, 2007, p. 53.

26 Bardgett, 'Remembering Srebrenica', p. 53.

27 For other examples of the transference of institutional knowledge or practices and of design techniques in Cambodia and Romania, see Rachel Hughes, 'Nationalism and memory at the Tuol Sleng Museum of Genocidal Crimes, Phnom Penh, Cambodia', in Katharine Hodgkin and Susannah Radstone (eds.), *Contested pasts: the politics of memory* (London and New York: Routledge, 2003), p. 181, and Michelle Kelso's contribution to this issue.

28 Daniel Levy and Natan Sznaider, 'The institutionalisation of cosmopolitan morality: the Holocaust and human rights', *Journal of Human Rights*, Vol. 3, No. 2, 2004, pp. 143–157.

29 See my discussion below of what Meierhenrich terms Rwanda's 'strategy of suffering vis-à-vis the international community'.

30 See Hughes, 'Fielding genocide', pp. 98–100; Jennie E. Burnet, 'Whose genocide? whose truth?: representations of victim and perpetrator in Rwanda', in Alexander Laban Hinton and Kevin Lewis O'Neill, *Genocide*: truth, memory and representation (Durham: Duke University Press, 2009), pp. 96–98; Guyer, 'Rwanda's bones', pp. 159–160; Rachel Ibreck, 'Remembering humanity: the politics of mourning' (PhD thesis, University of Bristol, 2009), p. 338.

31 Hughes, 'Fielding genocide', p. 98.

32 Tsitsernakaberd is an exception here, since the majority of the exhibition is entirely devoted to making a case for genocide in order to combat denial. One assumes that this is aimed at visiting dignitaries and tourists, since its Armenian visitors will hardly need convincing.

33 Hughes, 'Fielding genocide', p. 98.

34 Lars Waldorf, 'Instrumentalizing genocide: the RPF's campaign against "genocide ideology"', in Straus and Waldorf, *Remaking Rwanda*, pp. 48–66.

35 Guyer, 'Rwanda's bones', p. 159; see also Susanne Buckley-Zistel, 'Remembering to forget: chosen amnesia as a strategy for local coexistence in post-genocidal Rwanda', *Africa*, Vol. 76, No. 2, 2006, pp. 137–138; Burnet, 'Whose genocide?'.

36 See particularly Burnet, 'Whose genocide?', and Buckley-Zistel, 'Remembering to forget'.

37 See Meierhenrich, 'Topographies of remembering and forgetting', p. 290.

38 Meierhenrich, 'Topographies of remembering and forgetting', p. 292; Guyer, 'Rwanda's bones', p. 161.

39 Ledgerwood, 'The Cambodia Tuol Sleng Museum', p. 92. See also Alexander Hinton, 'Truth, representation and the politics of memory after genocide', in Alexandra Kent and David Chandler (eds.), *People of virtue: reconfiguring religion, power and moral order in Cambodia today* (Copenhagen: Nordic Institute of Asian Studies, 2008), pp. 68–69, 73–74.

40 Quoted in David Chandler, 'Cambodia deals with its past: collective memory, demonisation and induced amnesia', *Totalitarian Movements and Political Religions*, Vol. 9, Nos. 2–3, 2008, p. 356.

41 Chandler, 'Cambodia deals with its past', p. 356.

42 Hughes, 'Memory and sovereignty', p. 276.

43 Hughes, 'Fielding genocide', pp. 98–99.

44 Burcu Münyas, 'Genocide in the minds of Cambodian youth: transmitting (hi)stories of genocide to second and third generations in Cambodia', *Journal of Genocide Research*, Vol. 10, No. 3, 2008, pp. 419–421 ff.

45 Darieva, '"The road to Golgotha"', p. 103.

46 For a further discussion, see my forthcoming article 'Situating Tsitsernakaberd'.

47 Sarah E. Wagner, *To know where he lies: DNA technology and the search for Srebrenica's missing* (Berkeley and Los Angeles: University of California Press, 2008).

48 See Bain Attwood, 'Contesting frontiers: history, memory and narrative in a national museum', *reCollections: Journal of the National Museum of Australia*, Vol. 1, No. 2, 2006, pp. 103–114; Attwood, 'In the age of

testimony: the Stolen Generations narrative, "distance," and public history', *Public Culture*, Vol. 20, No. 1, 2007, pp. 75–95; Amanda Nettelbeck, 'The Australian frontier in the museum', *Journal of Social History*, Vol. 44, No. 4, 2011, pp. 1115–1128.

49 Useful here is Jeffrey C. Alexander, 'On the social construction of moral universals: the "Holocaust" from war crime to trauma drama', *European Journal of Social Theory*, Vol. 5, No. 1, 2002, pp. 5–85.

50 Ivan Zveržhanovski, 'Watching war crimes: the Srebrenica video and the Serbian attitudes to the 1995 Srebrenica massacre', *Southeast European and Black Sea Studies*, Vol. 7, No. 3, 2007, pp. 417–430.

51 Burnet, 'Whose genocide?'

52 Wagner, *To know where he lies.*

53 Timothy Ashplant, Graham Dawson and Michael Roper in their introduction to their edited volume *Commemorating war: the politics of memory* (New Brunswick and London: Transaction, 2000), pp. 3–85, distinguish between 'hegemonic' (publicly articulated) and 'sectional' (marginalized, subordinated, suppressed and/or oppositional) narratives; my definitions obviously differ slightly, since I am trying to encapsulate a (more fluid, less binary) public sphere in which many different interest groups with varying degrees of power construct their own narratives of the past. They may or may not be oppositional or suppressed, and the more hegemonic narratives may not be taken up by all.

54 Gabriel N. Finder, in his 'Yizkor! Commemoration of the dead by Jewish Displaced Persons in postwar Germany', in Alon Confino, Paul Betts and Dirk Schumann (eds.), *Between mass death and individual loss: the place of the dead in twentieth-century Germany* (New York: Berghahn Books, 2008), pp. 232–257, gives a broad-ranging analysis of these early or relatively 'spontaneous' (as they, too, were often enacted by committee) commemorations, noting also which endured and which faded as Israel and eventually other western nations established their own official commemorations.

55 Wagner, *To know where he lies*, note 16, p. 281 and pp. 70–74 for a general description and analysis.

56 Hughes, 'Memory and sovereignty', pp. 265–266.

57 Meierhenrich, 'Topographies of remembering and forgetting'.

58 There is a happy convergence with the preferred heroic symbolism of Soviet memorialization in a few of these memorials—in the villages of Musaler and Agarak, for example, both of which commemorate Armenian 'self-defence' (at Musa Dagh and Van). Otherwise, the memorials remain very abstract, since Armenian national suffering was not a narrative that fitted with the state's idea of commemoration. Interestingly (although not surprisingly), most of those built after 1991 take the same form—that of a *khachkar*, a traditional Armenian cross.

59 Meierhenrich, 'Topographies of remembering and forgetting', pp. 286–287. Original italics.

60 See Meierhenrich, 'Topographies of remembering and forgetting', pp. 284, 289.

61 Ledgerwood, 'The Cambodia Tuol Sleng Museum'.

62 Münyas, 'Genocide in the minds of Cambodian youth'.

63 Darieva, "'The road to Golgotha'", p. 98.

64 See, for example, Young, *Texture of memory.*

65 See Michael Meng, *Shattered spaces: encountering Jewish ruins in postwar Germany and Poland* (Cambridge, MA: Harvard University Press, 2011), and, for two photographic monographs exemplary of this searching, Jeffrey Gusky, *Silent places: landscapes of Jewish life and loss in Eastern Europe* (New York: Overlook Duckworth, 2003) and Chris Schwarz, *Photographing traces of memory: a contemporary view of the Jewish past in Polish Galicia* (Kraków: Galicia Jewish Museum, 2005).

66 Stuart Hall, 'Encoding/Decoding', in Simon During (ed.), *The cultural studies reader*, 3rd edn. (Abingdon: Routledge, 2007), pp. 90–103.

Memorializing colonial genocide in Britain: the case of Tasmania

TOM LAWSON

Britain is a post-genocidal state, although it (not surprisingly) has no official means for the memorialization of its colonial genocides. Britain cannot, however, be simply considered amnesiac about its genocidal past, which it has informally memorialized across various cultural genres. This article explores this observation through a case study of the ways in which the genocide of Indigenous Tasmanians has been remembered and indeed memorialized. Accounts of the genocide of Indigenous Tasmanians have been a consistent feature of British museum, literary and academic culture since the 1830s. As such, British engagement with genocide in Tasmania offers an interesting example of how genocide can be incorporated into national narratives that rely on neither victimhood nor denial. This is a particularly appropriate case study because Indigenous Tasmanians were universally represented as victims of a British 'extermination' in the metropole from the outset. Travellers wrote home with tales of violence from the 1820s, and Indigenous Tasmanian communities were constructed as a memory of the stone age from this point onwards. The decline of the Indigenous population appeared in diverse media: in fine art, in parliament and in print, often as a means to celebrate British sophistication and humanity. This article will offer an analysis of all of these colonial discourses, and argue that these enduring memories speak to a stable imperial identity in Britain which was, and continues to be, strengthened rather than undermined or disrupted by the allegation of genocide.

Introduction

It is a common accusation that Britain does not acknowledge the crimes of its Empire; that Britons are therefore insufficiently aware of the violence and brutality with which the British Empire was constructed and sustained.[1] This despite widespread acknowledgement that such violence includes incidences of genocide.[2] At first glance it is difficult to disagree. Certainly there appears to be very little public reflection in the British present on genocide in the British past. Notwithstanding Michael Rothberg's instruction that we see the connectedness of the memories of the Holocaust and colonial violence,[3] there seems little prospect of ubiquitous Holocaust memorialization encompassing sustained reflection on any other genocide any time soon, let alone one that occurred in the British world. Indeed, in a controversial draft of the national curriculum for history in England published at the beginning of 2013, the government implicitly contrasted the 'unique evil' of the Holocaust with an Empire constructed simply as Britain's gift to the world.[4]

It might therefore be assumed that to consider the manner in which one of those incidences of genocide from the imperial past, in Tasmania, has been memorialized in Britain would be to face silence. Certainly, if we look for formal memorialization or commemoration then that is indeed the case—you will find no physical memorials to destroyed communities from Tasmania or anywhere else in the former metropolitan centre of Empire. But there is more to memorialization than the performance of memory rituals or the deliberate effort to play homage to the dead. With regard to the destruction of Indigenous peoples and communities in Tasmania, what we can see is a kind of informal memorialization, which, like the physical presence of gravestones or memorial sculptures, finds a didactic purpose for both the memory of the dead and an understanding of their destruction. Throughout and across many different genres of representation in British culture since the 1820s, Indigenous Tasmanians and importantly their (wholesale) destruction have been used to underpin a repeatedly articulated version of British identity that emphasizes British superiority. It is my contention here that this is a form of memorialization, albeit one that is not often acknowledged.

It is therefore not the case that the atrocities of the Empire in Tasmania have not been remembered. This memorialization has often been submerged in British culture, but it can be found nonetheless. What is more, it has been present since genocidal violence and then sustained cultural destruction was visited on Indigenous Tasmanians by representatives of the British state. What follows is therefore essentially a case study in the manner in which a *perpetrator* society can construct positive narratives about its role in a genocide. What I uncover is not the denial of the genocidal impacts of British imperial expansion, which is perhaps the kind of inverse memorialization one might expect in a perpetrator state and society. Instead, we find the incorporation of those genocidal impacts into a series of different narratives, all of which underscore positive articulations of British identity. I will try and demonstrate this by considering a number of different representations of Indigenous Tasmanians in British culture since the beginning of the nineteenth century, which use the memory of the dead for the purposes of the present.

The use of the term genocide in application to Tasmania, or anywhere in Australian history, is contested, and in fact would be disputed by scholars coming from a number of different ideological directions.[5] Time and space do not allow for an extended discussion of the utility or otherwise of the term here. It suffices to say that I find it appropriate for two main reasons that I will briefly explore.

First, and perhaps most importantly, from the 1820s onwards the British themselves identified the impact of their presence in what they called Van Diemen's Land in terms that we would understand as genocide. In Britain, the government certainly believed that settlers were engaged in the extermination of Indigenous peoples in the 1820s and into the 1830s.[6] That sense endured across the rest of the century and in some ways up to the present day. In the article that follows, then, I will detail the importance of the self-identification as perpetrators of genocide in British culture. In those terms the accuracy or otherwise of the term genocide to describe the history of settler Indigenous relations is not strictly relevant. Put simply, it appropriately characterizes what Britons understood at the time.

However, the destruction wrought in colonial Van Diemen's Land/Tasmania can and should be understood as genocide. From the outset the British established, as Tony Barta phrased it, 'relations of genocide' in the society they built.[7] There was a genocidal consensus that united all representatives of British state and society in the view that there was no future for Indigenous people in the colony. This consensus included those who wished to exterminate Indigenous people, and those who in their own terms wished to 'protect' them (both from the savage settlers and from themselves). On its own terms, 'protection' would only have been successful if Indigenous people succeeded in transforming themselves into God-fearing British subjects. In addition, when they did not do so, the British developed a further narrative that understood Indigenous destruction as pre-ordained and natural, augmenting their already developed identity as the extirpators of Indigenous backwardness.

Finally, a note on sources. What follows is a study of British cultural engagement with genocide in Tasmania. Especially in the (post)modern era, cultural production is increasingly transnational and it is difficult to disentangle *British* representations from any other when narratives and images can be instantly transmitted around the globe. I have therefore limited myself to discourses that are distinctively British or cultural products deliberately created for a British audience or which had a particular impact in Britain. This means that there are what might appear to be notable gaps in the discussion. There is, for example, no engagement with some important texts in Australian historiography which self-evidently contribute to the general memorial discourses around genocide in Tasmania, and in particular there is little engagement here with the protagonists in the public struggles that became known as Australia's 'history wars' at the turn of the twentieth into the twenty-first century. It is not my claim that such debates had no impact in Britain, but they were seldom engaged with as an issue *for* Britain; rather they were overwhelmingly presented and reported as part of Australia's process of coming to terms with its past.[8] Such distance and disengagement obviously tells us much about the way in which the memory of British atrocities in Empire might be avoided but my focus here is on the way stories about Empire are and were related to Britishness rather than on such absences.

Furthermore, in outlining the memorial narratives around Tasmania in British culture, I am also inevitably engaging with the debate surrounding the importance of the Empire in the everyday lives of Britons in the nineteenth and twentieth centuries. Bernard Porter has famously argued that Empire was relatively unimportant, that Britons were 'absent minded imperialists' only dimly aware of, for example, the violence done in their name.[9] Porter equally maintains in his critique of my work on Tasmania (of which this article forms a part) that the evidence for sustained British engagement with genocide is too fragmentary to justify the conclusion that violence against Indigenous Tasmanians really had any significance at home.[10] Regrettably, a detailed study of the reception of the kind of ideas that I outline here eludes any scholar. Neither I nor Porter can really know what individuals thought when they read about murdered Tasmanians in the press, or saw their bodies and belongings exhibited in British museums. However, what follows does demonstrate the sheer consistency of the narrativization of genocide across time and space in Britain. Since the 1820s, Britons have been given stories of genocide in Tasmania that speak to their superiority and British imperial purpose. The consistency of the shape and texture of these stories suggests that we can at the very least identify a tendency to domesticate and memorialize colonial violence in an understanding of what it meant to be British. While I do not know what the people reading these stories thought of them, that the ideas within them are so similar and so consistently articulated suggests to me that they are more than just the unnoticed fragments of a conflict far, far away.

Narratives of destruction

The violence that contributed to genocide in Tasmania was discussed in Britain as it was occurring. During the 1820s the colony of Van Diemen's Land underwent massive demographic and indeed territorial expansion. Increasing numbers of free migrants from Britain (as well as convicts) drove a territorial expansion which brought colonists into conflict with an Indigenous population that sought to resist the usurpation of their land and the disruption of their traditional ways of life. The conflict became increasingly violent after 1824, leading to war and the rapid depopulation of the Indigenous nations.[11] The violence in the colony was explained in the metropolitan centre of Empire using two complementary narratives which begin to show how the memory of genocide was used in Britain from the moment destruction began.

The first narrative proposed that the Indigenous community were engaged in an irrational and insatiable campaign of revenge. This was based on a reading of the Risdon Cove massacre, in which an indeterminate number of Indigenous people had been killed when first encountering the nascent colonial settlement in 1804. Although that incident had gone unnoticed in Britain at the time, by the 1820s it was appearing in the popular press as explanation for the developing violence in the colony now.[12] The second explanation for violence, again related to the Risdon Cove massacre, was that it was the result of purely settler savagery. According to this interpretation, the settlers had somehow deviated from the British imperial purpose, and embraced violence in the pursuit of colonial conquest.[13]

Evidently these two narratives interacted. Both involved the implicit contrast between the violent and irrational Indigenous Tasmanians, the violent settlers and the noble British. Indeed, in a narrative that would be remade in several different ways across the nineteenth century, the British government consistently suggested that their Empire was the *solution* to the problem of violence in Van Diemen's Land rather than its cause. London repeatedly urged that its colonial government in Hobart intervene to restrain the violence of both settlers and

Indigenous clans. As such, from the outset understanding of the conflict in Van Diemen's Land and the attendant destruction of Indigenous communities was constructed in a manner that supported a vision of British moral and ethical superiority over both Indigenous resistors and the colonial settlers themselves.

These narratives were not confined to government. In the 1830s violence in Van Diemen's Land was being played out on the London stage as well as in newspapers and emigration propaganda.[14] William Moncrieff's popular opera, 'Van Diemen's Land', performed in 1831, presented a familiar message of conflict between the Indigenous population and British savages, in this case the convicts. In Moncrieff's fantasy the respectable settler population (those who properly articulated the British colonial vision) allied with Indigenous Tasmanians against the escaped convict population or bushrangers. Again a contrast was drawn between the benign British and the savage settlers (notwithstanding the intellectual leap involved in rendering some settlers no longer British).[15]

Playing on British understandings of Indigenous Australians, the central character in Moncrieff's drama was Bennelong. Bennelong had been brought to London in 1793 from New South Wales and had for two years been 'adopted as a pet of the officer set'.[16] In the play although not in reality, after his return, Bennelong travelled to Van Diemen's Land where he became a leader of Indigenous resistance. By indicting the convict population, Moncrieff's drama alleged that Britain had, through transportation, exported its vices. In this sense it was part of a critique of colonialism. Yet at the same time it was a defence of colonialism too. Ultimately in the play Bennelong was able to join forces with the respectable (and thus in these terms still British) settler population to repel the bushrangers that were terrorizing both Indigenous and settler communities. As such, it offered a vision of a co-operative future for colonialism, although it is a common future that might have come too late for the Indigenous population of Van Diemen's Land, who Bennelong acknowledged in the play were being 'extirpated'.[17] The memory of the dead was therefore being used here to highlight (perversely) the beneficence of Empire. Niall Ferguson used much the same logic in his history of *Empire* at the beginning of the twenty-first century, in which he argued that, had it not been for the British, genocide would have spread much further than Van Diemen's Land.[18]

Of course by the time of Moncrieff's opera, the idea of harmonious co-existence between the settler and Indigenous populations was just a fantasy. The colonial government, with the support of London, had effectively declared war on Indigenous peoples in Van Diemen's Land through Martial Law in 1828. The military approach legitimized violence against Indigenous people but it did not bring an end to their resistance, particularly from the Big River and Oyster Bay groups. That resistance was eventually nullified by a series of negotiations that were led by the evangelical George Augustus Robinson, and performed by his Indigenous guides. At the beginning of 1832, the Indigenous clans, of whom there were now only a few hundred survivors, together decided to desist from a conflict that had devastated them. By this stage it must have been clear to them that the only alternative was annihilation. The survivors were deported from Van Diemen's Land, eventually to the outlying Flinders Island.[19] Such action was again supported by the narrative that this was the best manner in which the Indigenous population might be protected—with obvious undertones regarding the protective arm of the British Empire.[20] By 1847, there were fewer than fifty Indigenous Tasmanians alive on Flinders Island and the community was sent back to the Tasmanian mainland. When William Lanne, the 'last' Indigenous Tasmanian man, and Truganini, the 'last' Indigenous Tasmanian woman, died in 1869 and 1876 respectively the entire Indigenous population of Tasmania was declared extinct.

A dying race?

As well as the idea that the British might protect the Indigenous population from violence, another narrative was emerging in the mid 1830s—namely that, whatever the efforts of the British, the Indigenous population were inevitably bound for extinction. This was another example of memorialization of the dead in a hymn of self-worship. Such a narrative could be found in diverse cultural genres. Take the example of emigration propaganda, designed from the beginning of the 1820s to entice migrants to the new world. The sunlit colonial future that emigrants were promised did not include the Indigenous population. Where they were represented, Indigenous Tasmanians were constructed as a people without culture.[21] Grotesque racial characterizations of the 'inferior' Tasmanian abounded.[22] Such images of the Indigenous population might have raised alarm, or been off-putting to potential migrants, as might the universal view that the Indigenous Tasmanians were (after Risdon) implacably hostile to their 'new neighbours'. Yet such concerns could be set aside, because the idea that the population was 'rapidly diminishing' abounded too.[23] These were a people of the past, hurtling towards oblivion. It was widely assumed that only the British would see the future in Van Diemen's Land.

The dying race idea was also exhibited in London's thriving art scene in 1835 through the paintings of the popular landscape artist John Glover. Again Glover's narration of the idea of Indigenous extinction constructed a very clear sense of the British as the men of the future. Glover had emigrated to Van Diemen's Land a few years previously and sent a number of paintings back to London for the 1835 exhibition. The paintings suggested a clear contrast between the Indigenous population of Van Diemen's Land who represented the island's past and the colony that represented its future. Glover's rendering of the 'colonial picturesque' has been praised because of the manner in which he captured the intensity of a 'hot Antipodean noon',[24] a phrase that evokes something of the quality of the light in his Tasmanian landscapes. Glover also painted Indigenous groups but he invariably presented them in shade, or gloomy twilight. Apparently to Glover they were not able to share the sunshine of the bright new day he saw on the island. 'Glover's Aboriginals are dancing in the dark.'[25]

Perhaps the most striking of Glover's 'Aboriginal arcadias'[26] exhibited in London was the panoramic *Mount Wellington and Hobart Town from Kangaroo Point*, which featured Indigenous men, women and children dancing and swimming in a shadowed foreground, with Hobart bathed in sunlight behind. *Mount Wellington* was one of the only paintings in which Glover presented the direct juxtaposition of Indigenous and colonial life on the island on the same canvas and as such his efforts to contrast the Indigenous past and the colonial future were particularly stark here. Hobart Town stands as an impressive and regimented colonial port. Several boats, large and small, are in the harbour, evoking a sense of an imperial trading centre. If this is a hymn to the imperial future, then the contrast with the Indigenous figures in the foreground could not be clearer. As ever with Glover's representations, they appear in shade engaged only in the frivolities of a simple life, with most dancing around a fire. The painting is an allegory of the final transition from Indigenous to colonial Van Diemen's Land. The 'conventionally shadowed foreground of classical landscape' represents a civilization that is to be displaced by the uplands of imperial might behind it.

Glover's paintings amounted to a public discussion of the 'extirpation' of Indigenous Tasmanians in London.[27] Crucially, these representations of the Indigenous population of the island as past, as a memory, were being displayed in the centre of Empire at the same time that their removal from Van Diemen's Land was being completed. The idea that Tasmanians were somehow a dying race is commonly identified as the mechanism by which the destructiveness of European colonialism was rationalized as the century wore on.[28] John Glover's shadowed Indigenous Tasmanians show that such rhetoric was important for understanding and justifying the ethnic cleansing of Van Diemen's Land as it was being enacted too. Thus, such ideas did not just rationalize the memory of genocide, but helped explain genocide to its contemporaries.

By the 1840s the image of the decline of Tasmanians and other Indigenous communities in British culture had hardened significantly. The radical James Roebuck wrote unapologetically in his *The Colonies of England* in 1849 that:

> for the sum of human enjoyment to be derived from this globe which God has given us, it is requisite for us to pass over the original tribes that we find existing in the separate lands which we colonise ... When the European comes into contact with any other type of man, the other type disappears ... Let us not shade our eyes and pretend not to see this result.[29]

This new, harsher discourse was also adopted by figures who have been subsequently adopted into the English literary canon. Samuel Sidney and Charles Dickens led the way at the end of the 1840s into the 1850s. Sidney produced a number of influential works on Australia, and wrote regularly on the subject for Dickens' periodical *Household Words* in which he was scathing about the 'inferiority' of Indigenous culture, and especially the idea that settlers should face judicial investigation for violence against Indigenous peoples.[30] In essence, Sidney believed that extermination was inevitable, and thus questioned any effort to check this development. Dickens famously attacked what he saw as the humanitarian idealization of the 'noble savage' in June 1853, in a furious denunciation that amounts, to use twenty-first-century language, to a call for genocide. Dickens wrote that it was 'highly desirable' that 'the savage' was 'civilised off the face of the earth ... and the world will be all the better when his place knows him no more'.[31]

A year later, Dickens confirmed his belief in the immutable categories of civilization and savagery in another famous article for *Household Words* in which he investigated the death of Sir John Franklin. This narrative was also linked to Tasmania, and tangentially to genocide. Franklin had been a former governor of Van Diemen's Land. He had taken an Indigenous Tasmanian (now known in popular culture as Mathinna) into his home and his wife had collected at least one Indigenous skull from Flinders Island. After leaving Tasmania, Franklin had returned to polar expeditions and had died in the Arctic in 1847. Dickens' account of his death dismissed the idea that a figure of such unimpeachable 'fortitude, sense of duty, courage and religion' could have resorted to cannibalism as had been reported in popular accounts of his demise.[32] After all, cannibalism was the defining identifier of the savage, who in Tasmania Franklin had sought to civilize. For Dickens, it was unthinkable that such a figure could himself have 'gone native' as the differences between such populations were fixed.

A decade later, Dickens' unapologetically exterminationist rhetoric was repeated by Anthony Trollope. Trollope's guides to emigration to Australia and New Zealand demanded that his English readers face the logic of their colonial impulses and thus their progress too. Colonization was, in Trollope's estimation, a theft of land, and involved the necessary diminution and then destruction of the original owners of that land. However, he was not prepared to declare this to be morally wrong because it engendered the spread of civilization and indeed had enabled Europeans to export their surplus population and now increased the wealth of the mother country. That this had been done at the expense of Indigenous communities was not for Trollope a matter of regret (and nor was it in reality, he conjectured, a matter of regret for the humanitarian philanthropists that he mocked) but simply a matter of reality. His strict sense of racial hierarchy meant that he regarded the replacement of an Indigenous population as a positive good.[33] In what again we would have to characterize as a call for genocide, Trollope wrote: 'of the Australian black man we may say certainly that he has to go. That he should perish without unnecessary suffering should be the aim of all who are concerned in this matter'.[34]

While Trollope's language was extreme, it was simply a development of a progress narrative that celebrated British triumph. It was in that sense no coincidence that such sentiments were articulated by men regarded as radicals and liberals. It was also not a coincidence that it was a rhetoric that developed out of humanitarian concern, the echoes of which can be detected in Trollope's desire to alleviate 'unnecessary suffering'. His call for elimination was just another form of, or perhaps even just a development of, the kind of evangelicalism that saw colonization as the means to extinguish barbarism or to save the 'savage'. Such rhetoric also relied on a celebration of liberal Britain, a sanctification of the British state as the only admissible route to the future. When Indigenous Tasmanians appeared, by the British's own estimation, to have proved that they were unable to accept lessons in civilization, then Trollope's rhetoric of destruction was the inevitable end-point. After all, there was little in the discourse of humanitarianism that suggested the possibility of an enduring Indigenous culture. As *The Times* leader writer wrote in November 1851, the Australian colonies now 'offered the spectacle of savage man cowed and overawed by the influences of a civilization which he can neither comprehend nor resist, and awaiting in harmless and listless inaction that speedy extinction to which some untraceable cause has doomed him'.[35]

Indigenous Tasmanians and their decline were then a contributor to a vision of the world that understood that settler colonization had a 'fatal impact' on Indigenous culture. When Tasmanians, and other Indigenous communities, failed to accept the worth of that settler civilization, or when they resisted it, such actions became further evidence for the inevitability of their demise. Such was the starkness of the contrast between the decline of Indigenous civilizations and the apparent forward march of Britain that in an entirely self-fulfilling cycle the impact of settler colonies became further evidence for the integral progress of British culture and society.[36] Genocide thus underpinned a more aggressive vision of the world that saw the eradication of Indigenous society itself as a self-evident good.

It would be quite wrong, however, to argue that the apparent passing of Indigenous Tasmanians did not evoke some disquiet in Britain. Accounts of Tasmanian decline were frequently an exercise in melancholia. *The Times* declared with a regret tinged with pride that 'we have exterminated the race in Van Diemen's Land'. In doing so, the leader comment rejected the idea that the cause of that extermination was some form of inevitable doom, and asked that Britain look again at the nature of its colonization.[37] James Bonwick's widely publicized account of the destruction of the Indigenous Tasmanian community echoed such requests and demanded the re-opening of debates on the nature of Empire and responsibility for Indigenous peoples when it was published in 1870.[38]

Bonwick's was the most detailed representation of the destruction of Indigenous Tasmanians on offer in mid- to late nineteenth-century Britain. Indeed, in London, the publication of *The last of the Tasmanians* was a literary event. As well as being widely reviewed, public readings were staged and in general it did cause the kind of reflection on the nature of Empire that the author desired. In many ways it brought together several of the fantasies and myths that had surrounded British understanding of the 'extermination' of the Indigenous community in Van Diemen's Land across the previous century. And in that sense Bonwick's book was also a product of those cultures of understanding—it was both an anguished cry at the fate of Indigenous peoples, and yet in essence a defence of the colonial idea and the system that had precipitated that destruction.

Bonwick went further than the general discourse by recognizing Indigenous agency during the 'Black War', referring, for example, to 'Aboriginal heroism' in the defence of their land. Yet for the most part he relied on traditional narratives. He argued that the Risdon Cove massacre had been the original offence that precipitated Indigenous violence,[39] and that it was the nature of colonial society and the character of the settlers that was the root cause of destruction (rather than the idea of colonization itself). Van Diemen's Land had become a 'dust-hole for the reception of the moral rubbish and turpitude of Europe' and had been occupied without consideration of the rights of the 'inhabitants of the island'.[40]

Yet while Bonwick's book was outwardly a critique of the nature of the colonization of Tasmania (if not the colonial idea itself), it also conformed to a familiar colonial discourse. Bonwick did criticize the agents of destruction in Van Diemen's Land, but he also constructed them in a familiar mode: the all-powerful men of modernity that were let loose on their helpless and hapless quarry. If Bonwick was ultimately sympathetic to the Tasmanian community and culture, he also conformed to a vision that it had simply been swept away by the might of the British Empire—the 'laughing' children of nature were no match for industrial man. 'We came on them as evil genii', Bonwick wrote, and 'blasted them with the breath of our presence'.[41] It was common for even those critical of the Empire and its impact on Indigenous communities to seek refuge in such imagery with which the likes of Dickens and Trollope would also have been comfortable. 'English speaking men are destined to cover the planet', wrote *The Times* in 1869, 'squeezing other races out of existence . . . the aboriginal Tasmanians have actually vanished'.[42] The celebration of the might of the Empire, and mourning for its impacts, were, therefore, melded together.[43]

The reception of Bonwick's book suggests that the wider reading public may not have shared his angst at the destruction of Indigenous Tasmanian society. More often than not Bonwick's work was received as a kind of extended colonial curiosity, the literary equivalent of the bones on display in various museums. And the story told in this 'curious work' was certainly understood to conform precisely to the received narrative of Tasmanian extinction or 'the pathetic story of their attempted civilization and the gradual extinction of their race'.[44] Bonwick was understood to be confirming the wider critique of Australia as a deviant society that strayed from the British purpose in the world—as the *Morning Post* conceded, 'it was a great misfortune to the aborigines of . . . Van Diemen's Land that the men who came to settle among them were chiefly of a class expatriated for their offences against the laws of this country'.[45] The impact (and intention) of such rhetoric was to protect the colonial ideal itself and Bonwick's repetition of this well-worn narrative was thus considered little more than a footnote to the more significant history of British expansion. As one reviewer noted of a later edition, Bonwick's was a history of the 'saddest episode in the civilization of the pacific coasts', but a little too large for the 'relative importance of the story to the vast congress of the British Empire'.[46]

Remembering genocide and the idea of race

Bonwick's understanding of Indigenous Tasmanians as a relic from a lost past reflected their position within race science too, especially within the prominent and indeed existential debate on the origins of the human race. In these debates, members of the Indigenous community of Van Diemen's Land, which had by

1870 been all but destroyed, were frequently portrayed as having been survivors from a previous era, often literally as an example of stone-age man. These assumptions were also popularized in British museum displays, sometimes up to the present day. Crucially, the idea that Tasmanians had been exterminated—in other words, that there had been genocide—was central to this discourse.

Coming from the abolitionist discourse that insisted on the common roots of all mankind, evolutionary biology and anthropology contributed to a vision of man progressing to civilization in the latter half of the nineteenth century—and of course Europeans were placed at the apex of this vision of development. It was claimed that the 'lower' races, like Indigenous Tasmanians, were peoples without culture who had been lost to development. According to John Lubbock, an associate of Charles Darwin's, to study Indigenous Tasmanians was to have access to a primitive society and therefore to 'penetrate some of the mist which separates the past from the future'.[47]

While men like Lubbock believed that in Indigenous society they were seeing a version of themselves in the past, a glimpse of the 'drift and cave men' of Europe,[48] there was an alternative discourse that denied the common root of mankind. For example, Robert Knox instead argued that race was a much harder characterization and delineated different species of men. Knox as a consequence foresaw a dark future, defined by racial conflict because it was impossible for different races to 'mingle', and as such, as the 'Saxon' spread across the globe, the 'sure extinction' of 'dark races' would follow. Again an understanding of the Tasmanian past was central to Knox's vision: 'Already in a few years we have cleared Van Diemen's Land of every human aboriginal. Australia, of course, follows.' Knox's embrace of genocide as the natural law of inter-racial contact was also predicated on a sneering rejection of 'philanthropic' attempts to civilize the 'darker brethren' as a 'war . . . against nature'.[49]

At first glance it might appear that it is only the overt racism of Knox (or Dickens or Trollope) that had accommodated genocide into a worldview. Yet the liberal discourse which had in the 1830s and 1840s advocated that 'lower races' could be transformed and civilized (in places like the settlement on Flinders Island) had fewer and fewer advocates as the century progressed. Indeed those that advocated protection and 'civilization' projects by the later 1800s were chiefly concerned with supervising the destruction of 'Aboriginal races' in the manner Trollope advised, of making their disappearance from the earth and journey into history and oblivion as painless as possible. The idea that Tasmanians and other Indigenous Australians represented a kind of pre-historic hangover certainly allowed liberals to come to terms with the destruction in Tasmania more readily, because it could then be represented as a natural and inevitable process. As J. G. Wood reflected on the demise of Indigenous Tasmanians in his *Natural history of man*, a popular publication that had originally appeared as a weekly serial, '[f]or the real cause we must look at the strange but unvariable laws of progression. Whenever a higher race occupies the same grounds as a lower, the latter perishes, and whether animate or inanimate in nature, the new world is always built on the ruins of the old'.[50]

As such, genocide in Tasmania became an important element in the progress mantra of the age for liberals as well as more hard-edged racists. Charles Darwin had first observed the decline of the Tasmanian population in his Beagle voyages. Coming from the same abolitionist tradition as the philanthropists of the Aborigines Protection Society, he too had been unwilling to declare the 'extinction' of 'Aboriginal' races inevitable in earlier publications. By the beginning of the 1870s Darwin's position had hardened, and he used the example of Tasmanians in *The descent of man* in his account of the evolutionary progress of culture and as such the inevitable destruction of 'Aborigines' in the face of ascendant, triumphant, liberal man.[51] Like other monogenists, Darwin's account of man's progress from a common root both relied on and explained the destruction of Tasmanians; in a liberal age it was also a means with which philanthropists could come to terms with their violent national past.

This debate about the nature of man and human origins went far beyond a narrow professional discourse between scientists. It was represented in school textbooks and displayed to the public in a variety of museums. By 1900, visitors could see the remains of Tasmanians in the Pitt Rivers museum in Oxford, the Hunterian Museum of the Royal College of Surgeons and the Natural History Museum in London. In the twentieth century, what was believed to be 'King Billy's Skull'—the skull of William Lanne—was displayed at the Anatomy Museum at the University of Edinburgh. The Department of Anatomy at Cambridge also reported excitedly that it had acquired a Tasmanian skull, one of the 'last representatives of Paleolithic man' at the beginning of the twentieth century.[52] Within that context, anthropologists regretted the 'unhappy fate' of the Tasmanians while collecting specimens of their remains as survivors from 'pre-history'.[53]

The Natural History Museum in particular had an important cultural presence. Its acquisition of human remains was reported in the press,[54] and it commanded over 400,000 visitors a year.[55] From 1899 those visiting the zoological mammals gallery would have seen a variety of representations of Tasmanians, including skulls displayed to demonstrate the smaller brain capacity of the 'lower type' of man, and a full skeleton. Adopting a Darwinian monogenist approach to racial science the Natural History Museum left their visitors in no doubt about what had happened to the 'aboriginal inhabitants of Tasmania ... now unfortunately exterminated'.[56] The idea of 'extermination' was central to all of these representations. Genocide was used as decisive confirmation of the 'inferiority' of Indigenous Tasmanians and thus the superiority of the British. The use of the remains of the dead as trophies to represent such narratives is a form of memorialization too.

The consistency of this discourse is striking. Tasmanian skulls were displayed in the Natural History Museum, in the same manner as they had been since 1899, until at least the 1950s. Consider too the example of the shell necklace that was on display in the Royal Albert Memorial Museum in Exeter until 1997. This was first acquired by the museum in 1933 and was reported in a local newspaper as a 'pathetic relic of a vanished people' who were in the 'same condition as the

European men of the older stone age'.[57] When it was finally removed from display (in order to be returned into the care of the Tasmanian Aboriginal Centre), the display 'remembered' that 'the natives [of Tasmania] were unable to comprehend new European values [after the invasion]. They could neither oppose nor conform, and they drifted into listless serfdom. It is not hard to see why Aboriginal culture is now the province of history'.[58]

The myth of extinction

The idea that Indigenous Tasmanians had been *completely* destroyed was also central to this discourse. This is a particularly tenacious myth. In the late 1970s, for example, Tom Haydon and Rhys Jones' controversial film about Truganini, *The last Tasmanian*, was broadcast on British Television.[59] The film was contemporarily controversial in Tasmania because it implied that Truganini had literally been the 'last' Tasmanian, and as such denied the aboriginality of the contemporary Tasmanian Aboriginal community. In Britain, such a discourse was absent. One letter writer to the *Radio Times* described his reaction: 'I am ashamed to be British and Christian. In comparative terms it [*The last Tasmanian*] made Hitler's extermination programme seem small-time as the *entire* Aboriginal population was annihilated in the most despicable way'. Newspapers, television and radio would continue to repeat the idea that in Tasmania, under the British flag, 'the colonists went on man-hunting safaris till there were no Tasmanian's left'.[60] Examples that rely on the idea of complete extermination can be found up to the beginning of the twenty-first century too. Ian Hernon labelled the 'Black War' one of 'Britain's forgotten wars' in a narrative that ended: 'in barely seventy years an *entire* race has been driven to extinction. It is a stain which has never been removed from the banners of the British Empire'.[61]

The idea of total extermination relied on and articulated an understanding of race as a fixed, immutable and biological characteristic that allowed it to ignore the presence of an enduring 'Aboriginal' community in Tasmania. The presence of such communities was not unknown in Britain; they were regularly reported in the British press or in travel accounts of Tasmania.[62] But because they were mixed race and as such not regarded as (to use the contemporary parlance) 'full blooded', they were not allowed to disrupt the idea that *all* Tasmanian Aborigines had been destroyed. After all, as well as articulating a biological understanding of race, the myth of complete extermination also spoke to the sheer extent of British power. It was in that sense part of the discourse that continued to deny the right of Indigenous communities to exist.

The idea of Aboriginal extinction was a common trope of accounts of Tasmania in travel literature in the first half of the twentieth century. The absence of Tasmania's Indigenous population was routinely referenced in these travelogues—as if it somehow added to the exotic allure of this remote location.[63] Yet if racial conflict was a way of confirming the otherness of Tasmania, the absence of Indigenous Tasmanians was also used to suggest the similarities between Tasmania and England and as such the completeness of the colonial victory over the Tasmanian wilderness. George Porter's *Wanderings in Tasmania* reflected, for example, on the success with which the colonists had transplanted English culture, at the same time as marvelling at the 'careless' extermination of the 'amazingly primitive and pathetic' Tasmanians. Again the idea of extermination was used to construct a sense of racial hierarchy—one culture had been destroyed, while another had successfully transplanted itself to the other side of the world.[64] Nearly 150 years later, Jeremy Paxman wrote very similarly that Indigenous Tasmanians had disappeared after a 'trial of strength with citizens of the most technologically advanced nation on earth'.[65]

The myth of extinction was also important for another discourse that came from an alternative political direction to much of the material I have surveyed, in the sense that it was overtly critical of British imperialism. There has been a consistent strain of anti-imperial politics and scholarship in Britain that has used genocide in Tasmania to highlight the iniquities or indeed the lie of British imperial progress. The most iconic example is H. G. Wells' references to Tasmania in the preface to *War of the worlds*, first published in 1898. Wells compared his Martian invasion to the British treatment of 'one of the "inferior races"', '[t]he Tasmanians in spite of their human likeness entirely swept out of existence in a war of extermination waged by European immigrants'.[66]

But Wells' example is instructive and suggests that we ought not to be too sentimental about the characterizations of genocide constructed by the critics of Empire. Whatever the force of Wells' critique, he seems to have accepted the veracity of the idea of racial inferiority, too. In *The outline of history* he had described Indigenous Tasmanians as 'paleolithic'.[67] Indeed Wells used, in *War of the worlds*, the idea of genocide as an indicator of that inferiority. And Wells has been accused of racism elsewhere. He certainly flirted with English eugenicists, and as such was operating a very similar sense of the implications of genocide in Tasmania for the understanding of racial hierarchy that defined the spirit of his age.[68]

In the aftermath of the Second World War, and in the era of decolonization, the idea of genocide in Tasmania did become a kind of rhetorical failsafe in the critique of Empire by British scholars. V. G. Kiernan's *The lords of human kind*, for example, described the genocide in a knowing rhetorical flourish as a '*final solution*'.[69] Kiernan's use of language is interesting, and bears out to an extent Michael Rothberg's claims about the interactions of Holocaust memory and that of colonial genocide.[70] But these allegations of genocide were rarely well contextualized. As such, these critical narratives had a tendency to infantilize (or worse) Indigenous Tasmanians as the helpless quarry of the modern and all-powerful exterminationists. Critiques like Kiernan's emerged from and remained within a discourse that accepted and indeed further embedded the idea of Indigenous Tasmanian racial inferiority, based on an understanding of their destruction.

Such an account suggests a possible relationship between contemporary claims that the events in Tasmania were genocide and the myth of extinction. Are contemporary historians, including myself, simply repeating the extinction myth when they cite Tasmania as an example of genocide? As Rebe Taylor and

Ann Curthoys have observed, Australian scholars in particular have at times avoided the characterization of Tasmania's colonial past as genocide in order to be able to prioritize Indigenous Tasmanian cultural survival.[71] The idea of genocide, it seems, might have been understood as a barrier to the message of the Tasmanian Aboriginal community that declared loudly *we are alive*. Certainly, as will be shown, there was no cultural sensitivity to the idea of Aboriginal survival in Britain in the later twentieth century and as such there is a relationship in wider culture between the idea of genocide and the myth of extinction. Yet it does not necessarily follow, as both Taylor and Curthoys argue, that the idea of genocide must incorporate the claim of total extinction, although the latter is important for wider cultural conceptions of colonial Tasmania operating in Britain right up to the present day. Where genocide scholars do repeat the myth of extinction it can be legitimately argued that they are perpetuating the very ideas that helped rationalize extermination in the first instance.

Remembering genocide and the return of human remains

Recently, the idea of extermination combined with a memorial lament for the lost Tasmanians has been crucial to debates over the return of human remains and Tasmanian cultural property from British museums. Genocide, and particularly the idea of complete extermination, was used to construct a narrative of superiority within these discussions by some members of the British museum community.

Since the mid 1970s, the Tasmanian Aboriginal Centre has campaigned for remains stolen from Indigenous graves in the nineteenth century to be returned. This was a process that began in relation to remains held in Tasmania itself, and then spread to the rest of the world. The remains held in UK institutions have been subject to requests to return since the mid 1980s. The most symbolic of these was the demand for the return of 'King Billy's Skull' from the University of Edinburgh, which was successfully negotiated in 1991. The most recent were the protracted discussions around the repatriation of remains from the Natural History Museum in 2007.

It could be argued that the process of returning remains from the UK to Tasmania is itself evidence of a kind of 'coming to terms with the past' in Britain, an acceptance of the historic injustices of colonialism and an attempt to begin atonement. After all, and thanks in part to the campaigning of the Tasmanian Aboriginal Centre, all major institutions in the UK now have policies that recognize the right of Indigenous communities to the remains of their ancestors. The UK government recognized the ethical imperative to return, and indeed all Tasmanian human material has now been repatriated.

Yet further consideration of the discourses surrounding these issues suggests that British connections with its genocidal past were not being fully confronted or overcome in these debates. In fact, the degree to which some articulations of identity remain anchored in a rather familiar colonial discourse is striking, as is the degree to which they are reliant on the memory of genocide in Tasmania. Consider first the original decision to return 'King Billy's Skull'. It was not reached easily. At first, the University of Edinburgh refused the request. Vigorous arguments against return were proposed within the university community and a binary opposition between the 'moral, political and cultural' case for return, and the 'scientific' arguments against it, was constructed (this is not to say that there was not an equally vigorous argument proposed for return within the university community; there was, and what is more, it won). Those arguing against return perpetuated the characterization of Indigenous populations as irrational in comparison to the rational, enlightened and scientific West.[72] One of the last acts of the scientific community that argued against return was to declare that 'King Billy's Skull' held by Edinburgh had been proven not to be that of William Lanne—an apparently desperate attempt to assert the certainty and superiority of western science over Indigenous Tasmanian faith.[73]

Since the return of 'King Billy's Skull' there have been vigorous arguments for retention put forward publicly by the representatives of institutions such as the Natural History Museum and the University of Cambridge. These have effectively adopted the enlightenment position (as articulated by their forebears in the nineteenth century) that they were (are) carrying out research for the benefit of all humanity, and as such were able to represent the universal good. In the words of Robert Foley, director of the Centre for Human Evolutionary Studies at the University of Cambridge, 'these [indigenous Tasmanian] skeletons are an irreplaceable record not just of particular cultures and populations, but of humanity as a whole'. What is more, Foley claimed that the descendants of those people in the present demanding return would themselves prefer to see such remains retained by museums as 'a part of global heritage, and as a source of historical and scientific ideas and discoveries'.[74] Similarly, the director of the Natural History Museum declared in 2003 that he could not consent to the idea that only an ethical case could be made for the return of remains because that ignored the universally conceived 'public benefits' of scientific research into remains.[75]

This conception of the universal benefits of science, and indeed the presumption that scientists could speak for all humanity, gives some indication of the *colonial* nature of the debate about remains in the public sphere. Consider Robert Foley's argument that Indigenous communities themselves should want remains to be retained for 'science'. Foley suggested, quite rightly, during a debate in May 2003 organised by the Institute of Ideas, that the desire to return remains was historically contingent—a postcolonial articulation of identity that sought to right the wrongs of colonial injustice. Foley stated:

> I think you should also remember that in the future, future generations both of ourselves and Indigenous communities may well look back if all this material has all disappeared and wonder what has happened to their history. They'll want to be, as they're hopefully given greater access to education and the wealth that goes with development then they will want to see this preserved in the same way as ... that we enjoy discovering about our pasts through television programmes and going to museums.

Such claims were suffused with assumptions that would not have been out of place in the original colonial exploitation of Van Diemen's Land. Foley not only represented western science as the natural outcome of human progress, but assumed that all other peoples will 'through development' become, in effect, like 'us'. As such, the (self-declared) scientific perspective on the return of remains was an argument for an ongoing colonization.

It is not just in these progress-laden assumptions that arguments in favour of retention appeared to reflect colonial positions, which in turn indicate the endurance of some nineteenth-century assumptions. Debates about the return of Tasmanian remains in the UK have also consistently returned to the idea that Indigenous Tasmanians had been entirely destroyed. It was present in the University of Edinburgh's discussions around King Billy's Skull,[76] and was invariably a part of later debates around return in the public sphere too. Again Robert Foley argued that the University of Cambridge was unable to return any of its three Tasmanian skulls because there was no genetic community to which they could be returned: 'the Tasmanians no longer exist, and can have no descendants'.[77] A group of UK museums also raised the idea of extermination as a practical barrier to return in their submission to the government working group of the early 2000s:

> A further problem has been the possible lack of mandate vested in those individuals representing repatriation. In particular, to remove particular genotypes from the possibility of scientific investigation is akin to a form of racism if not genocide, because those genotypes would be excluded from important ways in which we may continue to investigate or define our species.[78]

Such claims operated an entirely biological or genetic understanding of the idea of race, and as such suggest that the death of race science may have been somewhat exaggerated.[79] In fact, the Tasmanian Aboriginal Centre characterized such sentiments as reminiscent of the Nazi era.[80] They are certainly a clear example of the relationship between the idea of total extermination and enduring dispossession.

In another response to the government consultation on repatriation, it was claimed that although the circumstances of the collection of remains were unacceptable, we should acknowledge and indeed celebrate that such material was saved: 'had our predecessors not been so inquisitive and so organised, then this material ... would have been lost forever'.[81] Such a narrative involved a clear evasion of the violence involved in collection. Most remains in the UK were taken from graves at Flinders Island, where Indigenous Tasmanians had been deported under threat of force following a campaign of violent dispossession. William Lanne's skull had been stolen while his body lay in a Hobart morgue in the aftermath of his death.

It is also difficult to escape the conclusion that such statements implied the same wonder at the apparent power that the idea of extermination bestowed on the colonists themselves:

> the extermination of the Aboriginal Tasmanians (genocide) is an appalling crime and amongst the worst atrocities of colonialism. Ironically, in this case, the facts render demands for the repatriation of remains of Tasmanian origin empty. Strictly speaking the Tasmanians were a geographical isolate and have no descendants to claim their relatives.[82]

The logic of such claims was clear: 'we' (that is the western scientists) won the right to control of these remains through 'our' wholesale destruction of the Indigenous community. Human remains were in that sense memorials to 'our' triumph.

Conclusion

Those commentators who assert that Britain is amnesiac of the violence of its colonial past are of course partially correct. Despite the ritualistic references to extermination that have been reviewed here, it would be difficult to argue that genocide in Tasmania (or anywhere else in the British world) is prominent in popular consciousness. But the endurance of that discourse of extermination suggests that it would also be wrong to argue that genocide is entirely absent too—the eruptions into public discourse reviewed above are too regular and too uniform. In fact, they reflect a sense of significance that has become embedded in some articulations of British identity that seem to use genocide as evidence of superiority and which still give voice to the assumptions about Indigenous inferiority that underpinned the desire to, at the very least, expunge Tasmanian culture from the face of the earth in the first instance.

Although there is no physical memorial to those people and cultures destroyed by the British Empire, and no formal memorial rites are practised for them in Britain, it is simply not the case that there has been no memorialization. In a series of memorial laments across different cultural genres, the memory of Indigenous Tasmanians and particularly their destruction has been utilized in the construction of a particular version of being British. This is not an identity that either avoids or denies the destructiveness of the British Empire in Van Diemen's Land, but one that embraces it. In Holocaust studies, we are familiar with the idea of efforts to 'master' or make 'usable' the past. The manner in which Britons have been invited to remember genocide in Tasmania is truly an example of the 'mastery of the past'. The memory of violence is, as we have seen, used as evidence of British superiority.

Endnotes

1 See, for example, George Monbiot, 'How Britain denies its holocausts', *Guardian*, 27 December 2005. Retrieved from http://www.monbiot.com/2005/12/27/how-britain-denies-its-holocausts/.

2 See, for example, Niall Ferguson, *Empire: how Britain made the modern world* (London: Penguin, 2004), pp. 108–109.

3 Michael Rothberg, *Multidirectional memory: remembering the Holocaust in the age of decolonization* (Stanford: Stanford University Press, 2009), p. 7.

4 See, for example, David Cannadine, 'The future of history', *Times Literary Supplement*, 12 March 2013.

5 The most obvious example is Keith Windschuttle, *The fabrication of Aboriginal history* (Sydney: McLeay Press, 2002). Henry Reynolds, *An indelible stain? The question of genocide in Australia's history* (Melbourne: Penguin Australia, 2001) also dismisses the idea of genocide. Indigenous Tasmanian scholars have also rejected the term, largely because it is bound up with the myth of total extermination in Tasmania and does not allow for sufficient emphasis on the enduring survival of an Indigenous community. This is discussed in detail in Rebe Taylor, 'Genocide, extinction and Aboriginal self-determination in Tasmanian historiography', *History Compass*, Vol. 11, No. 6, 2013, pp. 405–418. Nicholas Clements, *The Black War: fear, sex and resistance in Tasmania* (Brisbane: University of Queensland Press, 2014) is the most recent example

of an account of colonial violence that, following Henry Reynolds, rejects the idea of genocide in the Tasmanian context: Henry Reynolds, 'Genocide in Tasmania', in A. Dirk Moses (ed.), *Genocide and settler society: frontier violence and stolen indigenous children in Australian history* (New York and Oxford: Berghahn Books, 2004), pp. 127–149.

6 Hence the famous warning from the Secretary of State for the Colonies that any policy geared towards the destruction of Indigenous peoples in Tasmania would 'leave an indelible stain upon the character of the British Government' in 1830. Reynolds, *An indelible stain?*, p. 4.

7 Tony Barta, 'Relations of genocide: land and lives in the colonization of Australia', in Isidor Wallimann and Michael N. Dobkowski (eds.), *Genocide and the modern age: etiology and case studies of mass death* (Westport: Greenwood Press, 1987), pp. 237–251. Barta also notes that the Imperial British government understood the destructiveness of their policies in his '"They appear actually to vanish from the face of the Earth": Aborigines and the European project in Australia Felix', *Journal of Genocide Research*, Vol. 10, No. 4, 2008, pp. 519–539.

8 In the *Independent on Sunday*, 19 April 2009, in an article confronting the absence of Aboriginal names on Australian war memorials, Kathy Marks wrote of 'white Australians' struggle to come to terms with their colonial past'. Typically, although the article was concerned with Australian history under British rule, this was not confronted. Similarly Philip Knightly in the *Independent on Sunday*, 7 May 2000, wrote: 'it remains one of the mysteries of history that for nearly two centuries *Australia* was able to get away with the crimes *it* inflicted on the Aboriginals' (emphasis added).

9 Bernard Porter, *The absent-minded imperialists: what the British really thought about Empire* (Oxford: Oxford University Press, 2004).

10 Bernard Porter, 'How bad are we?', *London Review of Books*, Vol. 36, No. 15, 2014, pp. 36–37.

11 For a narrative of increasing violence, see Lyndall Ryan, *Tasmanian Aborigines: a history since 1803* (Sydney: Allen & Unwin, 2012), pp. 74–150. See also Tom Lawson, *'The last man': a British genocide in Tasmania* (London: IB Tauris, 2014), ch. 2. For the most comprehensive account of the Black War, see Clements, *The black war*.

12 *Morning Post*, 14 November 1821.

13 This is the heavy implication of much government correspondence between London and Hobart over the matter at the end of the 1820s. See A. G. L. Shaw (ed.), *Van Diemen's Land: copies of all correspondence between Lieutenant Governor Arthur and his majesty's secretary of state for the colonies, on the subject of the military operations lately carried out against the Aboriginal inhabitants of Van Diemen's Land* (Hobart: Tasmanian Historical Association, 1971). The most famous is the letter sent from the then Secretary of State for the Colonies on 5 November 1830 that warned that the 'extinction' of the Indigenous population of Van Diemen's Land would leave an 'indelible stain' upon the character and reputation of the British government.

14 For a general analysis of the role of emigration propaganda in Britain, see James Belich, *Replenishing the earth: the settler revolution and the rise of the Anglo-world* (Oxford: Oxford University Press, 2009).

15 See W. T. Moncrieff, *Van Diemen's Land: an operatic drama in three acts* (London: Thomas Richards, 1831).

16 David Sampson, 'Strangers in a strange land: the 1868 Aborigines cricket tour and other Indigenous performers in mid-Victorian Britain' (PhD thesis, University of Technology, Sydney, 2000), p. 72.

17 Moncrieff, *Van Diemen's Land*, p. 37.

18 Ferguson, *Empire*, p. 108.

19 The best account of the genocide is contained in Henry Reynolds, *Fate of a free people* (Melbourne: Penguin Australia, 2004), although Reynolds would reject the label.

20 See, for example, the correspondence between London and Hobart in which the Secretary of State for the Colonies expresses admiration for the policy adopted on Flinders Island. Goderich to Arthur, 21 June 1832, National Archives, Public Record Office, CO 408, Vol. 9.

21 George William Evans, *History and description of the present state of Van Diemen's Land, containing important hints to emigrants* (London: John Souter, 1824), p. 25.

22 Mrs Augustus Prinsep, *The journal of a voyage from Calcutta to Van Diemen's Land, comprising a description of that colony during a six months residence* (London: Smith, Elder & Co., 1833), p. 79.

23 *Hampshire Telegraph*, 29 December 1823.

24 David Hansen, *John Glover and the colonial picturesque* (Hobart: Tasmanian Museum and Art Gallery, 2003), p. 98.

25 David Hansen, 'The picturesque and the Palawa: John Glover's Mount Wellington and Hobart Town from Kangaroo Point', in Timothy Barringer, Geoff Quilley and Douglas Fordham (eds.), *Art and the British Empire* (Manchester: Manchester University Press, 2007), p. 51.

26 Ian McLean, *White Aborigines: identity politics in Australian art* (Melbourne: Cambridge University Press, 1998), p. 41.

27 Glover exhibited thirty-six Tasmanian landscapes in Bond Street in July 1835, including several that featured Indigenous groups. The exhibition catalogue noted that Indigenous Tasmanians were 'now nearly extirpated'. *A catalogue of pictures descriptive of the scenery, and customs of the inhabitants of Van Diemen's Land, together with views in England and Italy painted by John Glover esq.* (London: publisher unknown, 1835).
28 For a brilliant analysis of the dying race thesis, see Patrick Brantlinger, *Dark vanishings: discourse on the extinction of primitive races* (Ithaca: Cornell University Press, 2003).
29 Quoted in Brantlinger, *Dark vanishings*, p. 6.
30 Coral Lansbury, *Arcady in Australia: the evocation of Australia in nineteenth century English literature* (Melbourne: Melbourne University Press, 1970), pp. 63–72.
31 Charles Dickens, 'The noble savage', *Household Words*, 11 June 1853.
32 Charles Dickens, 'The lost Arctic voyagers', *Household Words*, 2 and 9 December 1854.
33 Anthony Trollope, *Australia and New Zealand* (London: Chapman and Hall, 1873), p. 60.
34 Trollope, *Australia and New Zealand*, p. 76.
35 *The Times*, 19 November 1851.
36 Russell McGregor, *Imagined destinies: Aboriginal Australians and the doomed race theory 1880–1939* (Melbourne: Melbourne University Press, 1998), p. 20.
37 *The Times*, 30 December 1864.
38 James Bonwick, *The last of the Tasmanians, or The black war of Van Diemen's Land* (London: Sampson, Low, Son & Marston, 1870).
39 Bonwick, *The last of the Tasmanians*, p. 36.
40 Bonwick, *The last of the Tasmanians*, p. 324.
41 Bonwick, *The last of the Tasmanians*, p. 57.
42 *The Times*, 29 July 1869.
43 Brantlinger, *Dark vanishings*, p. 2.
44 *Daily News*, 18 October 1869.
45 *Morning Post*, 24 December 1869.
46 *The Pall Mall Gazette*, 15 May 1884.
47 John Lubbock, *The origin of civilisation and the primitive condition of man: mental and social condition of savages* (London: Longmans, Green & Co., 1870).
48 James Backhouse Walker, *The Tasmanian Aborigines* (Hobart: John Vail, 1900), p. 1.
49 Robert Knox, *The races of men: a philosophical enquiry into the influence of races over the destinies of nations* (London: Henry Renshaw, 1862), p. 229.
50 J. G. Wood, *The natural history of man: being an account of the manners and customs of the uncivilised races of men* (London: George Routledge and Sons, 1870), p. 68.
51 Charles Darwin, *The descent of man and selection in relation to sex* (London: Penguin, 2004), pp. 212–221.
52 Cressida Fforde, *Collecting the dead: archaeology and the reburial issue* (London: Duckworth, 2004), p. 69.
53 Henry Ling Roth, *The Aborigines of Tasmania* (Halifax: F. King & Sons, 1899), pp. v–vii.
54 *The Times*, 28 July 1899.
55 William Stearn, *The Natural History Museum at South Kensington* (London: Heinemann, 1981), p. 393.
56 Natural History Museum, *Guide to the specimens illustrating the races of mankind* (London: Natural History Museum, 1908), p. 33.
57 This comes from a fragment of a local newspaper (title unrecorded) held in the archive of the Royal Albert Memorial Museum. No reference, but held in the files concerned with the return of Truganini's necklace and dated 21 October 1933.
58 From a photograph of the display provided by the Royal Albert Memorial Museum.
59 It was broadcast on BBC2 on 23 May 1978. *Radio Times*, 20–26 May 1978, p. 39. Many thanks to James Jordan for this reference.
60 *The Guardian*, 23 September 1987. For other examples, see John Spurling's play *The British Empire*, which was staged in Birmingham in 1980 and broadcast on BBC Radio 3 in 1982; and *The Observer*, 28 November 1982. For a more contemporary newspaper reference to the 'complete genocide of the Aborigines in Tasmania', see *The Guardian*, 15 August 1997.
61 Ian Hernon, *Britain's forgotten wars: colonial campaigns of the 19th century* (Stroud: Sutton Publishing, 2003), p. 296 (emphasis added).
62 See, for example, the detailed account of the population of the Furneaux islands in *The Times*, 23 September 1890. This population was still being reported on some half a century later. See *The Times*, 23 April 1946.
63 See, for example, 'Lord Northcliffe on Tasmania: ideal holiday place', *The Times*, 22 September 1921.
64 See George Porter, *Wanderings in Tasmania* (London: Selwyn and Blount, 1934) and the review of that publication in *The Guardian*, 25 October 1934.
65 Jeremy Paxman, *Empire: what ruling the world did to the British* (London: BBC Books, 2011), p. 145.

66 H. G. Wells, *War of the worlds*, edited by Patrick Barrinder and notes by Andy Sawyer (London: Penguin Classic, 2005), p. 9.
67 Wells, *War of the worlds*, note 10, p. 188.
68 John Sutherland, 'Devil take the hindmost', *London Review of Books*, Vol. 17, No. 24, 14 December 1995, pp. 18–19.
69 V. G. Kiernan, *The lords of human kind: European attitudes to the outside world in the imperial age* (London: Penguin, 1972), p. 277 (emphasis in the original).
70 Rothberg, *Multidirectional memory*, p. 7.
71 Taylor, 'Genocide, extinction and Aboriginal self-determination', pp. 410–414; Ann Curthoys, 'Genocide in Tasmania: the history of an idea', in A. Dirk Moses (ed.), *Empire, colony, genocide: conquest, occupation and subaltern resistance in world history* (New York: Berghahn Books, 2008), pp. 229–252.
72 See 'Extract from a paper discussed at a meeting of the University Court on 5 November 1990'. Supplied to the author by the University of Edinburgh.
73 Appendix D1 (2), Extract from Senatus Minutes, University of Edinburgh, 5 December 1990. Supplied to the author by the University of Edinburgh.
74 Robert Foley, 'Should human parts in museums be returned to their place of origin? No', *BBC History Magazine*, July 2003.
75 See 'Statement of dissent from Neil Chalmers', reprinted in *Care of historic remains: a consultation of the working group on human remains* (Department for Culture, Media and Sport, 2004), pp. 62–68.
76 See, for example, the debate on the issue in the university court, where the senior management of the university had cautioned that it needed to be 'borne in mind that the Tasmanian Aboriginals were now extinct'. Extract from Minute of Court held on 9 July 1990.
77 Quoted in *The Observer*, 28 September 2003.
78 Cited in Fforde, *Collecting the dead*, p. 159.
79 See Gavin Schaffer, *Racial science and British society, 1930–62* (Basingstoke: Palgrave Macmillan, 2008) for a detailed interrogation of the endurance of race science.
80 Department for Culture, Media and Sport, *Report of the working group on human remains* (2003), p. 53.
81 Department for Culture, Media and Sport, *Report of the working group on human remains*, p. 38.
82 Department for Culture, Media and Sport, *Report of the working group on human remains*, p. 38.

Site of memory and dismemory: the Valley of the Fallen in Spain

ANDREA HEPWORTH

This article focuses on the Valley of the Fallen in Spain as both a site of memory and dismemory. The monument at Cuelgamuros was constructed as a burial site for the Francoist fallen and the commemoration of their victory between 1940 and 1958 with the help of forced labour, consisting of thousands of Republican prisoners. Not only did many of these prisoners suffer serious injuries or death, but, in addition, thousands of Republican remains were exhumed from mass graves throughout the country, transferred and anonymously interred at the Valley in 1959 over and above the authorized burial of Francoist bodies. The destruction of the mass graves in the process, as well as the transfer of the bodies, was instrumental in disguising committed atrocities, and must be viewed as an attempted 'mnemocide' of the Republicans. The interment of dictator Francisco Franco's remains in 1975 at the basilica of the Valley certainly highlights the contested nature of this memory site. In this discussion, it will be argued that the Valley of the Fallen represents a site with blurred distinctions between a mass grave, a monument and an unacknowledged site of suffering for Republican prisoners, whose memories and stories continue to be silenced and unacknowledged at the site. The article will focus on the 'dissonant heritage' of the Valley, which has become a focal point of controversies and debates in recent years. It will further be argued that the unacknowledged 'heritage of violence' of the Valley has transformed the site into a contested *lieu de mémoire*, and that debates about and clashes at the Valley of the Fallen reflect conflicts rooted in the past dictatorship and still existing in contemporary Spain.

Introduction

Seventy-five years after the end of the Civil War and nearly thirty-nine years after the end of the Franco dictatorship in 1975,[1] debates on historical memory, the recuperation of the past and how to deal with the legacies of the Franco regime and the transition to democracy are still fiercely ongoing in Spain. In fact, since the late 1990s, Spain has experienced an outpouring of memories about the recent past in a variety of forms, including radio and television programmes, books, documentaries and films. This 'memory boom' follows decades of a silencing of past injustices not only during the dictatorship, but also in the immediate post-Franco period to enable a peaceful transition to democracy. This tacit agreement forged by the political elites has often been called the 'pact of silence' or 'pact of oblivion'. Instrumental in the shift from silence to intense public debates were, on the one hand, the emergence of different models of peaceful transitions in nations such as South Africa, the former communist countries of Eastern Europe and various Latin American countries, which demonstrated that a peaceful transition was not dependent on collective amnesia; and, on the other hand, the coming of age of the grandchildren's generation with their greater temporal distance from the traumatic past that allowed them to break the silence and start to reclaim historical memory.[2]

Campaigns to locate and exhume Republican mass graves, largely spurred by organizations such as the Association for the Recovery of Historical Memory (ARMH) founded in 2000,[3] further instigated cultural, political and historical debates and brought previously silenced stories of repression into the public arena. In particular, the use of video testimony at burial sites may be viewed as a first step towards a working through of the traumatic past; the mediatization[4] of the investigative exhumation process certainly opened up a new discursive space for the traumatic memories of the past in Spain. It is estimated that 30,000 bodies, mainly of Republicans killed during the Spanish Civil War and the Franco dictatorship, still lie in unmarked graves. The approximate death toll of the Civil War (1936–39) is said to be around 500,000: about 200,000 are estimated to have died in battle and another 200,000 men and women were executed behind the lines; an unknown number were killed in bomb attacks and as a result of evacuations from territory conquered by the Nationalists.[5] A further 440,000 Republicans went into exile and of those about 10,000 perished in Nazi concentration camps.[6] After Franco's victory, about 20,000 more Republicans were killed and many others died of malnutrition and disease in overfilled prisons, concentration camps and work battalions.[7] Historian Paul Preston has controversially referred to the events in Spain during the Civil War and its aftermath as the 'Spanish Holocaust', thereby endeavouring to highlight the systematic nature of the atrocities committed during that time by placing Spanish suffering in a wider comparative context.[8]

In recent years, the *Valle de los Caídos*, or Valley of the Fallen, in Spain—a monumental memorial conceived by and built under Francisco Franco, and also his resting place—has become one of the points of convergence of heated debates, and this article will focus on the controversial site as both a site of memory and dismemory. It will be argued here that the Valley of the Fallen occupies an undefined space with blurred distinctions between a monument, a mass grave and an unacknowledged site of suffering for political prisoners during its construction and constitutes a contested and 'dissonant heritage'. The term 'dissonant heritage' was coined by John Tunbridge and Gregory Ashworth in acknowledgement of the contested nature of heritage;[9] the interpretation of heritage is deemed 'dissonant' when different groups assign different meanings and stories to a specific site, landscape or object, which causes disquiet, anxiety and often alienation. In addition, historic sites associated with violence of any kind imbue such heritage with strong emotions of repugnance, empathy or fascination,[10] which is clearly evident in the debates about the Valley of the Fallen, a site that has been managed as a cultural heritage site by the government agency Patrimonio Nacional since 1957. The additional dimension of the Valley of the

Fallen as an enormous mass grave further adds significance—and much controversy—to the site; cemeteries are 'powerful instruments for the transmission of heritage messages through death'[11] and the fact that the only named graves at the Valley are those of Falange founder José Antonio Primo de Rivera and former dictator Francisco Franco is a clear indication as to whose memory and heritage is preserved at the site.

The concept of 'dissonant heritage' is particularly fruitful for the analysis of contested sites of memory because it not only allows us to consider between which elements dissonance occurs, but also to classify the different types of dissonance and track the 'constant revision and change' that heritages undergo 'in response to the demands of the present',[12] evident in the changing official discourse regarding the site since its inception. The concept of heritage, and in particular dissonant heritage, is clearly related to the complex relationship between memory and history, which is particularly relevant with regards to traumatic events such as the Franco dictatorship that occupies a liminal space between history and memory.[13] It has long been recognized that historical accounts are an interpretation of the past in the present, and can never be fully representational of the past, because historians do not work with bare, un-interpreted facts.[14] Similarly, Maurice Halbwachs' concept of 'collective memory', which also informs this article, specifically refers to memory that is created and conveyed by social groups, emphasizing that human memory can only function within a collective context and thus different social groups will have distinct collective memories[15]; this is evident in the disputes surrounding the Valley of the Fallen. Hence history, collective memory and heritage all represent fragments of the past that are negotiated in the present, and are all relevant to this discussion.

This article opens with a historical overview of the system of forced labour introduced by the Franco regime, in order not only to outline its importance for the construction at Cuelgamuros, but also to highlight its punitive and repressive nature and who these measures were directed against. The importance of the monument for political identity formation under the Franco government and its use as a tool of political legitimization will further be discussed, in order to facilitate an analysis of its legacy. The article will further outline and explore the importance of the Valley of the Fallen as a burial site, not only for the most controversial remains of Franco and Primo de Rivera as discussed above, but also for the thousands of other often nameless bodies interred there, and the controversial debates and discussions surrounding this issue. Drawing on Harold Proshansky's concept of 'place-identity'[16] and Sharon MacDonald's notion of 'undesirable heritage',[17] a sub-category of 'dissonant heritage', the present-day effect of the Valley's material legacy will be examined and the continuities and changes at Cuelgamuros since Franco's death in 1975 will be critically evaluated.

In this discussion, Marianne Hirsch's concept of postmemory further informs the analysis of the continuing legacy of the Valley for contemporary generations and the changing official discourse over time.[18] Pierre Nora's notion of *lieux de mémoire*[19] and Benjamin Forest and Juliet Johnson's concept of 'glorified and contested' places of memory will also be employed to outline the shift of the status of the site in Spain's collective memory,[20] and Ricard Vinyes' notion of an 'ecumenical museum' will be discussed in the context of a plurality of memories towards the end of the article.[21]

The Valley of the Fallen, located fifty-eight kilometres from Madrid in Cuelgamuros, is the most visible and infamous legacy of the Franco dictatorship. It consists of a monastery, a cemetery and an imposing 150-metre high and forty-seven-metre wide cross towering over a vast subterranean basilica excavated from the granite rock. The monument was constructed with the help of forced labour between 1940 and 1958 as a burial site for the Nationalist fallen and as a site of commemoration and glorification of Franco's 'Crusade'.[22] In addition to the

Figure 1. Valley of the Fallen with the 150-metre high cross by Diego Méndez (copyright Andrea Hepworth)

authorized burial of Francoist bodies, thousands of Republican remains were dug out from mass graves and transferred to the Valley in 1959;[23] the transfer of the bodies also helped to destroy evidence and disguise committed atrocities.[24]

Repression and the system of forced labour in Francoist Spain

A system of forced labour was developed from 1937 onwards when it became apparent that the 1936 coup d'état would morph into a long war and an increasing number of Republicans were taken prisoner. In 1937, the Concentration Camp Inspectorate for Prisoners was set up, which was even in name reminiscent of Nazi Germany's Inspectorate of the Concentration Camps established in 1934.[25] Furthermore, Franco's decree of the bestowal of the right to work for prisoners of war coincided with the creation of the first forced labour battalions in 1937, which alleviated the financial burden of lengthy internment to the Franco regime.[26] In accordance with this, the Redemption of Prison Sentences through Labour Scheme was created in 1938 in which the prisoners were promised reduced sentences in exchange for performing work,[27] providing the regime—and private industry—with a cheap source of labour;[28] this scheme was instrumental for constructions such as the Valley of the Fallen. The decree establishing the scheme formed part of the judicial framework enacted to repress and persecute Republican supporters or any other 'enemies of the state'. Two of the laws central to this persecution were the Law of Political Responsibilities (LRP), enacted in 1939,[29] and the Law for the Repression of Freemasonry and Communism, passed in 1940.[30]

Political views were not the only factor that led to persecution under the Franco regime. Women were punished for not adhering to traditional roles, homosexuality was outlawed and judgement was passed on so-called moral qualities, with strict outward adherence to the Catholic faith demanded. Many people were arrested and executed without trial or sent to labour battalions; others were humiliated and persecuted. Some lost their jobs and income and even mourning a 'Red' was prohibited and punished; the repression and censorship was thus both physical and psychological. As a result, voices of Republican suffering were completely suppressed in the public sphere; their memories were hidden and repressed in the wake of a lone, standardized version of the Spanish Civil War.[31] Nationalist victims, on the other hand, were recognized and honoured; their bodies were exhumed and then reburied during elaborate ceremonies. Commemorative plaques were placed in crypts, cathedrals or places where Nationalist victims had died and sometimes streets or squares were named after them, which meant that the families could come to some kind of closure and mourn their dead openly. The Republican victims, in contrast, were not acknowledged, and their families were unable to grieve openly or mention their loss. All these measures made the defeated side pay financially, morally and socially for the reconstruction of Spain—a venture literally undertaken by the prisoners in Cuelgamuros in constructing a stone monument that enshrined the memory of the victors.

Forced labour at the Valley of the Fallen

At the end of 1943, some six hundred political prisoners were working in Cuelgamuros, transferred from various prisons.[32] The total number of prisoners who worked at the site during the entire phase of construction ranges in the thousands. However, like many other figures regarding the Spanish Civil War in general, and the Valley of the Fallen in particular, the number of political prisoners who worked at the Valley can only be estimated, and hence numbers vary.[33] This is one of the points of contention, or dissonance, raised by right-wing defenders of the status quo of the Valley, such as Juan Blanco, former deputy director of the right-wing newspaper *El Alcázar* and author of *Valley of the Fallen: neither political prisoners nor forced labour* (2009),[34] historical revisionist Pío Moa, César Alcalá and Pablo Linares, president of the Association for the Defence of the Valley of the Fallen (ADVC), among others. They dispute not only the total number of prisoners who worked at the Valley during the construction, but also the term 'forced labour' for these workers by citing the deduction in prison sentences and payment given in exchange for the prisoners' work. Moreover, they contend that prisoners volunteered to work in Cuelgamuros, and cast doubt on the workers' classification as political prisoners, claiming that many were 'common' prisoners.[35] However, prisoners who had engaged in military rebellion were often not classed as political prisoners, but 'common criminals',[36] and there was hence not a clear distinction between these two categories. Moreover, the categorization of 'common prisoner' is more than problematic when stealing food out of desperation could incur sentences of fifteen to twenty years.[37] Secondly, the mortality rate in prisons was extremely high due to illness and malnutrition in overcrowded conditions,[38] hence 'volunteering' to work outside the prisons was a question of survival, although conditions in labour camps were also notoriously hard.[39] It must certainly be conceded that prison sentences were reduced and remuneration occurred under the Redemption of Prison Sentences through Labour Scheme, although doubt must be cast not only on the justice of the sentence per se, but also on the equality of payment compared to free labourers.[40]

Another highly contested point is the death toll at the monument; it spans from fourteen given by the physician of Cuelgamuros to thousands reported by former prisoners who worked at the site.[41] The discrepancy in the numbers of deaths can be explained partly by the fact that injured workers who were transferred to hospitals ceased to be registered as Cuelgamuros prisoners, and their deaths were hence not linked to the construction site. In addition, many prisoners died later of silicosis, induced by the inhaling of pulverized granite produced by the daily explosions to dynamite the structure out of the mountains.[42]

The regulation and symbolic construction of cultural space under the Franco regime

In the 1940s and 1950s, monumental funerary structures were used throughout Spain to immortalize the memory and heroism of all those fallen for 'the fatherland and God'.[43] The Valley of the Fallen was the most eminent of these. Martyr and death cults are a common denominator of many totalitarian and fascist regimes; they were used as a propaganda tool to unite the masses behind state power.[44] The 'cult of the fallen' employed by the Franco regime, which culminated in the construction of these monuments, was invoked to create the 'imagined community' of the New Spain.[45]

Moreover, the building of the monumental sepulchre of the Valley was to assert the political authority of the new regime by referring back to its 'glorious past'.[46] These attempts at establishing a continuous link between a political regime and the historic past are called 'invented traditions' by Eric Hobsbawm, serving the purpose of legitimizing an institution or government.[47] The construction of the Valley was but one, albeit very strong, link in the legitimization process of the Franco regime. Its construction and function was incorporated and embedded in laws and cultural institutions created for propaganda purposes. The State Delegation of Press and Propaganda (DEPP), for example, dated back to 1937, a year prior to the introduction of the 1938 Press Law, which controlled cultural expression through censorship. Significantly, the DEPP was also in charge of all 'monuments, memorials, commemorative publications, celebrations and public art' of which the Valley of the Fallen would eventually form an essential part.[48] The symbolic cultural space of power was hence strictly regulated by the Franco regime, and the linking of art with propaganda was established early on.

It is contended by Brian Graham et al. that 'heritage is at the core' of the 'material, representational and symbolic activities' constructing place and identity;[49] the material legacy of Francoist legitimization attempts is still evident at the Valley and forms a focal point of dissonance and contention between contemporary left-wing and right-wing groups. One of the arguments disputing the 'negative heritage'—a 'conflictual site that becomes the repository of negative memory in the collective imaginary'[50]— of the Valley is the sole foregrounding of its religious, Catholic aspect in an attempt at its depoliticization.[51] The regime's emphasis on Catholicism is certainly evident at the Valley, most prominently by the enormous cross conceived by the architect of the Valley of the Fallen, Diego Méndez, and the adorning sculptures created by Juan de Ávalos.[52] The commissioned pieces are composed of a pietà above the portico of the entrance to the basilica, as well as two groups of sculptures for the base of the cross, consisting of the four evangelists and the four cardinal virtues. The combined weight of the sculptures exceeds twenty tonnes and their cost skyrocketed from a proposed nine to seventeen million pesetas upon completion in 1955.[53] The Valley of the Fallen was clearly an example of a 'co-opted or glorified monument', which Forest and Johnson define as memory sites that are either preserved or further extolled by the state, and to which substantial resources are allotted.[54] The decision to place monuments to the fallen throughout the entire country, then, was a conscious attempt to alter and shape Spain's collective identity and memory, for which the Valley of the Fallen was paradigmatic.[55]

An array of artists collaborated in the decoration of the 262-metre long basilica, the main feature of the Valley.[56] The entrance to the basilica is provided by a large bronze door, followed by high internal wrought iron gates. Behind the gates await two frightening archangels resembling warriors. The fact that they were cast from melted down cannons used in the Civil War only increases their palpable threat.[57] Furthermore, all six chapels branching off the nave are linked to aspects of the military history of Spain,[58] further evidence negating right-wing arguments of the site's exclusively religious character. At the most prominent spot, in front of the main altar, are the tombs of Franco and Primo de Rivera. Also noteworthy is the stone mosaic inside the cupola depicting a seated Christ surrounded by several groups of saints, martyrs and heroes. One of these groups is composed of civil and military Francoist victims of the Civil War, accompanied by a cannon and Falangist and Carlist flags. These components were rediscovered in 2009 and caused much controversy without, however, causing their alteration or destruction.[59] The dome of the basilica rises above the transept, from which the largest two chapels branch off. Large spaces for the remains of the fallen were created behind these chapels, which were divided into up to five levels. Similar spaces, with up to three levels, were created behind each of the other six chapels, and later, when filled with remains, walled up with brick and covered with granite.[60]

In August 1957, less than two years before the inauguration, the Foundation of the Holy Cross of the Valley of the Fallen was established by government decree, and the ownership of the territory of the Valley with all its buildings, furnishings and associated rights transferred to it. Furthermore, a subsequent 1958 agreement also incorporated the Benedictine abbey and made it subject to canonical law.[61] Of particular contemporary concern regarding the future of the Valley is the fact that the basilica and its interior is under the authority of the Church, while the government agency Patrimonio Nacional—and hence the state—has full authority over the rest of the Valley.

Further 'symbolic capital'—which Pierre Bourdieu describes as a form of symbolic wealth that helps dominant groups secure appreciation in public opinion for their activities and as such is closely related to the legitimation of power through symbolic form[62]—was added to the Valley by celebrating Nationalist commemorative days at the site, such as 18 July (the anniversary of the military uprising), 1 April (the 'Day of Victory') and 1 October (the 'Day of the Caudillo').[63] A Requiem Mass for all the fallen was celebrated on 20 November, the anniversary of Primo de Rivera's, and later also Franco's, death.[64] The regime hence attempted to establish new symbolic references not only by creating national holidays surrounding its military history, but also by foregrounding the Valley in their celebration. The three pillars of the regime—that is, its ideological Falangist-fascist base, the military and National Catholicism—were all represented in the Valley in various forms. The transferral of the bodies of the 'heroes and martyrs' was intended to complete the symbolic message of the monument. Before its inauguration in April 1959, however, it was discovered that there were insufficient Nationalist remains to fill the extensive space.[65] As a result, Republican bodies were dug up and also interred at the site, resulting in a more 'reconciliatory' message than initially intended. In a timespan of only two weeks, approximately ten thousand Republican bodies were transferred to the Valley in 1959, mostly without the consent and knowledge of their families.[66] Most of the transferred Republican bodies were treated, even in death, as second class 'nameless

Figure 2. Juan de Ávalos' pietà above the portico of the entrance to the basilica (copyright Andrea Hepworth)

Spaniards', whose remains were exhumed from mass graves and who remained anonymous.[67] The emptying and razing of mass graves certainly assisted in concealing the killings by obliterating evidence. There was, then, after the 'politicide', the 'elimination of a political class',[68] also the attempted 'mnemocide' of the Republicans, that is, the attempted erasure of their memory.[69]

The transfer of remains to Spain's largest Civil War mass grave—the Valley of the Fallen

Discussions about the organization of the impending transfer of bodies to the specifically constructed chambers in the basilica began in December 1957.[70]

However, the official announcement of the inclusion of Republican bodies, as well as establishing the only interment criteria as being Spanish and Catholic, only occurred in May 1958.[71] The beginning of an official discourse of reconciliation and the opening of Spain to the rest of Europe certainly influenced the promulgation.[72] This changed official discourse, presenting the Valley as a symbol of reconciliation rather than one of victory, takes centre stage in many arguments by the political right who claim that the Valley was planned from its inception as a burial site for all the dead of both sides of the Civil War,[73] which is clearly untrue. In view of this controversy, a closer look at the burials at the Valley is warranted.

Officially, 33,833 bodies are buried at the Valley,[74] although that number is disputed. The more realistic number of remains of victims, suggests José María Calleja, is between 40,000 and 70,000,[75] whereas Queralt Solé i Barjau meticulously points out the errors committed in the paperwork by the municipalities when sending remains to the Valley.[76] Documentation of the transfer of remains is held in two places: at the General Archive of the State Administration (AGA) in Alcalá de Henares, where most documents of the Department of Internal Affairs are housed, and at the Benedictine Abbey, where three record books are held.[77] Remains were requested and sent from most provinces in Spain; excavations took place at cemeteries and mass graves. Bodies were then sent either in individual coffins, if they could be identified, or in collective coffins; however, the number of dead was often estimated. Often skulls were counted to give an indication of the number of bodies, but there are cases where bones or skulls were left behind in mass graves, highlighting the unreliability of the figures.[78]

Upon arrival at the Valley, the information provided by the municipalities was, unchecked, entered into the record books, maintained by the monks of the Benedictine Abbey, and a separate index card containing additional information was created. There are, nevertheless, instances where the government source and the Benedictine record books differ, and the documentation held at AGA indicates that bodies were transferred to the Valley when, in fact, this did not happen.[79] The most significant of these cases concerns 11,000 bodies which had not been transferred from Paracuellos del Jarama due to the (Francoist) relatives not assenting to the reburial.[80] The 'martyrs of Paracuellos', killed by Republicans in the so-called Paracuellos Massacre during the Civil War, were supposed to add much 'symbolic capital' to the Valley of the Fallen. The lack of this significant number of corpses, which the regime had counted on, might have inspired the reburial of Republican bodies at Cuelgamuros,[81] rather than the wish for a reconciliatory common burial ground. Further doubt on the correctness of the figures is cast by the abbot of the Valley of the Fallen who admitted that there could be many more than those officially registered; he estimated the number as up to 60,000.[82] It is, furthermore, not only difficult to establish the exact number of those interred, but also the manner of death and which faction—Francoist or Republican—the dead belonged to, as well as the exact place of burial.[83] It is striking that the transfer of remains to the Valley continued until 1983, eight years after Franco's death in 1975.[84]

The 'undesirable heritage' of the Valley of the Fallen after 1975

The most controversial point of divergence in disputes about the Valley is the presence of Franco's remains in the basilica. In 1975, more than 100,000 people attended Franco's funeral at the Valley of the Fallen,[85] which affirms the site as a 'glorified monument' for Franco supporters. Although there is much debate over whether Franco had intended the basilica of the monument to be his final resting place,[86] the architect of the Valley, Méndez, asserts that this was the case.[87] Disturbingly, the procession following Franco's coffin to the Valley of the Fallen went past the same landscape that, two months earlier, some of the last prisoners to be executed under Franco traversed on their last journey from Carabanchel prison.[88] Clearly, the dissonant heritage of the monument lies not only in the monumental construction itself, but also in its significance as the tomb of the dictator who helped to design it. The fact that Franco's body was interred at Cuelgamuros certainly shows the lack of confidence in Spain's political stability after his death. The subsequent transition to democracy was based on a wish to avoid the recurrence of the traumatic events of the Civil War and to establish a political equilibrium between the various forces in order to implement and stabilize a democratic system. In particular the 1977 Amnesty Law, which granted immunity from prosecution for crimes against humanity for both those who had supported and those who had opposed the dictatorship, was instrumental in the 'negotiated burial of the past' during the transition, which avoided the confrontation of the collective trauma of its citizens.[89]

Due to the potential fragility of the fledgling democracy, the Valley of the Fallen remained untouched in the transition, as did nearly all other monuments and symbols in Spain during that period. Demolishing the symbols, memorials and statues of a repressive regime is usually one of the first acts undertaken after a regime change. However, none of this occurred at the Valley of the Fallen—neither in the immediate post-Franco period, nor in the more than thirty-nine years afterwards. Nevertheless, attempts to—at least partially—destroy the Valley have been made: one in 1962, another in 1999 by members of the left-wing First of October Anti-Fascist Resistance Groups (GRAPO) and the last in 2005.[90] These attempts at its destruction—significantly, two of these attempts occurred after the end of the dictatorship—demonstrate that the symbolic values the Valley stands for are not uncontested; the dominant collective memory is challenged by a counter-memory in the form of this attempted iconoclasm.

Cleary, the Valley of the Fallen represents an 'undesirable heritage', that is, heritage that might cause a predicament as to whether it 'should be destroyed or altered in order to obliterate' a traumatic past or 'to shape changing identities'.[91] The material legacy of the Valley of the Fallen will endure for many years to come and will affect the collective memory and identity of future generations. The multiple layers of the legacy of the Valley—that is, the monument itself, its unacknowledged heritage of violence and suffering for political prisoners during its construction, and the site as a mass grave—present an extremely difficult heritage for contemporary generations.

Distinctions such as those made by scholar Ulrich Winter, who views the exhumations at Republican mass graves as a '*lieu de mémoire* par excellence', representing the 'bursting of the past into the present',[92] and juxtaposes these with the Valley of the Fallen as a place of non-recognition and annihilation of the Other—the 'totalitarian counter-image' of a *lieu de mémoire*[93]—cannot easily be upheld when taking into account that the Valley itself contains the largest mass grave of the Spanish Civil War. The Valley exists in this undefined space with blurred distinctions between categories; it still functions as a *lieu de mémoire* to the victors, but it also represents a site of dismemory for those who suffered at the Valley—a fact that is still unacknowledged at the site—and whose anonymous remains were exhumed and buried at a location where the body of their victimizer now also lies.

The detailing and analysis of the writing out of Republican suffering in official guidebooks about the Valley of the Fallen is, to this article's author, the most valuable contribution of Gareth Stockey's 2013 English language volume on the site.[94] Stockey further developed Paloma Aguilar's earlier brief analysis of these guides and their difference in wording in their Spanish and English language versions.[95] This is of particular interest to an analysis of the changing official discourse of the site, not only in a temporal context, but also with regard to different target audiences. He places, quite properly, the Valley of the Fallen into the wider context of the 'memory wars' in contemporary Spain and also discusses the 'cultural universe of early Francoism'.[96] However, the material and cultural legacy and symbolism of early Francoism, as well as its legal framework, has been analysed in more depth by Dacia Viejo Rose in her work *Reconstructing Spain*, which was of great value to this article. The connection between National Catholicism and Franco's regime is a further focus of Stockey's work, in particular its manifestation in the Valley's art work; his wider analysis of the symbolism and use of the 'combined image of sword and cross'[97] not only in Spain but also in Britain is, however, not central to this article. On the other hand, the work's comprehensive discussion of contemporary debates and in particular the role of blogs and websites—left wing and right wing—develops a fascinating and in-depth overview of media involvement and importance in discussions about the Valley,[98] which is most relevant to the changing discourse of the site discussed throughout this article. A further interesting point raised by Stockey is the absence of the symbolic representation of women as 'active participants in the civil war', which further highlights that the Valley is not a 'monument to all the dead',[99] and that the symbolism at the site requires further contextualization.

Place-identity, collective memory and dissonant heritage

Proshansky argues that place-identity—that is, a certain self-identity bound to a place—is constructed on a conscious as well as an unconscious level, and hence heavily influenced by its surroundings.[100] Similarly, Halbwachs observes that collective memory is preserved in physical landscapes, and that, furthermore, the environment and its materiality also shape the collectives living in it.[101] It is clear that contemporary generations living with the material legacy of the dictatorship, such as the enormous mausoleum in Cuelgamuros, are impacted by it; the never-ending controversies surrounding it are ample proof of this. According to Winter, the importance and power of the Republican mass graves lie in their position at the intersection of the testimonial memory of the physical site and the transmission of communicative memory by witnesses and family members, as well as by cultural memory distributed through the media;[102] might the way towards dispelling the dissonance of the Valley's heritage lie in something similar? Might the diversification of interpretation strategies and mediatization be a way forward?

A further issue raised by scholars such as MacDonald addresses the question of whether a landscape specifically built for the purpose of generating 'senses of identity and feelings of enthusiasm that have since become widely regarded as problematic or reprehensible', such as the Valley of the Fallen, is able, if left unqualified and untouched, to inspire future generations to support movements such as fascism.[103] This is a pertinent issue to be considered regarding the Valley, where clashes between Falangists and Republicans still occur on commemorative Falangist days, such as 20 November, the anniversary of Franco's and Primo de Rivera's death. From 1976 onwards, celebrations on this day have included processions to the Valley, planned by right-wing organizations. Moreover, after the failed coup d'état attempt in 1981, the day and its demonstrations became part of the political calendar of European neo-Nazi groups.[104] Since the 1990s, there have been regular anti-fascist counter-demonstrations with clashes culminating at the Valley, although the numbers of right-wing demonstrators have declined over the years.[105] However, these clashes are an indication of the continuing impact of the dissonant heritage of the site.

Controversies at the Valley of the Fallen after the enactment of the Historical Memory Law

In 2007, in great part spurred by the historical memory movement and the nationwide exhumation of mass graves, the so-called Historical Memory Law was enacted. The law condemned the 1936 uprising and subsequent Franco dictatorship, recognized procedures for compensation for and recognition of the victims of the Civil War and Franco's repression, and mandated the removal of Francoist symbols, plaques and statues from public buildings (unless they possessed religious or artistic value). It further avowed state help to find, identify and exhume victims of the Franco regime, and forbade acts of a political nature or any exaltation of the Civil War, its protagonists or Franco at the Valley of the Fallen.[106] Unsurprisingly, the Historical Memory Law was highly controversial; for some it went too far and threatened to open old wounds, while for others it did not go far enough.

Due to the law exempting Francoist symbols from removal if they possess religious or artistic merit, symbolism connecting Franco's regime to the monument is still existent at the Valley. There are, for example, Francoist escutcheons adorning the façade and the entrance door, as well as huge Francoist crests carved in stone on both sides of the entrance arcade to the basilica, thus forming part of the building. Also inside the basilica, the coat of arms is still present at various points; in some instances it is carved in stone, in others it forms part of the furniture.[107]

Two years after the passing of the Historical Memory Law, the government decided to close the Valley to the public due to the delicate state of Ávalos' pietà. The closure was decried by right-wing groups and activists associated with the Benedictine order as a first step by the socialist government towards permanently closing the Valley and avoiding the controversies surrounding it,[108] and even as an attack on Christianity.[109] It is clear, then, that the site of the Valley of

Figure 3. Valley of the Fallen; Francoist escutcheon in the background (copyright Andrea Hepworth)

the Fallen now represents a 'contested site of memory'.[110] According to Forest and Johnson, at times of critical juncture, *lieux de mémoire* become sites of major conflict and will often suffer one of three possible fates, depending on 'changing official conceptions of national identity'.[111] As discussed above, the Valley started as a 'co-opted or glorified' site under the Franco regime. However, memory sites can also become 'disavowed'; these sites are either neglected and ignored, or actively destroyed by the state. The third category encompasses 'contested' memory sites, which are sites that are objects of political conflict and neither clearly 'glorified' nor 'disavowed'. The Valley clearly fits that profile in contemporary times; the time of critical juncture in question here, it could be argued, began with the 'memory boom' in the 1990s, followed by the enactment of the Historical Memory Law and subsequent crucial events, such as the first criminal investigation into crimes committed during the Spanish dictatorship in 2008, instigated by Judge Baltasar Garzón, in which the mass grave at the Valley's basilica was one of the first ordered to be opened.[112] Although the trial was stalled by the indictment of the judge for the violation of the 1977 Amnesty Law, since 2010 hundreds of Spanish victims have turned to an Argentinian court in search of justice.[113] The Argentinian case has gained momentum since late 2013 and has sparked many demonstrations and public debates.

These debates in the public domain were mainly instigated by members of the third generation, the so-called grandchildren's generation in Spain, and the effects of 'postmemory' are most certainly the driving force behind this. Hirsch defines 'postmemory' as 'the relationship that the generation after those who witnessed cultural or collective trauma bears to the experiences of those who came before'.[114] Hirsch suggests in particular that possibly 'it is *only* in subsequent generations that trauma can be witnessed and worked through, by those who were not there to live it but who received its effects, belatedly, through the narratives, actions and symptoms of the previous generation'.[115] A focal point of these controversies and debates was more often than not the Valley of the Fallen, which confirms its status as 'dissonant heritage' and contested site of memory.

As a result, the Association of Relatives for the Exhumation of Republicans at the Valley (AFPERV) was founded in 2011,[116] and in May of the same year a Commission of Experts for the Future of the Valley of the Fallen was set up. In response to some of the families who now wish to remove the remains of their relatives from the Valley and to give them a proper burial in the cemeteries of their villages, a medical examiner was engaged by the Commission to prepare a report on the viability of the identification of the interred bodies at the Valley of the Fallen. Water ingress at the Valley had resulted in the shifting of some of the remains from one chapel to another in 1990, without adequate documentation. Probably as a result of this, some of the chapels that should have contained remains were found empty; others had remains where there should not have been any. Many of the wooden boxes had disintegrated and the content of different columbaria was mixed with others. The report concluded that the exact number of remains could not be determined, and neither could the information of the Benedictine registry books regarding their placement be relied on; thus, the conditions of the remains, as well as their mixing, would make identification all but impossible.[117] Nevertheless, relatives allowed to accompany forensic experts on their visits to the Valley opined that the remains were not in as bad a state as officially declared.[118] It seems certain, however, that not all of the remains currently interred at the Valley of the Fallen will be able to be identified or disinterred, particularly given that some now form part of the structure of the building.[119]

In November 2011, the Commission of Experts for the Future of the Valley of the Fallen recommended the removal of Franco's remains and the conversion of the Valley into a site of memory for all victims of the Civil War. Furthermore, the urgent need for an information centre at the site was stressed, in order to place the site and its history into its socio-political context and to conduct further research into the history and identity of those buried at the Valley.[120] Moreover, the Commission emphasized the need for the addition of a strong didactic, explanatory component to Cuelgamuros, rather than its removal or destruction.

The recommendation to remove Franco's remains from the basilica caused much controversy. The reburial was vehemently rejected by Franco's daughter and many right-wing supporters such as Linares, whose argument centred again on the 'symbol of reconciliation' the Valley had supposedly formed since its inception and who—correctly—pointed out that the state had no authority over the interior of the basilica, including the remains, due to it being subject to canonical law.[121] On the other hand, relatives of the Republican victims buried at the basilica expressed their repugnance over victims and victimizers lying in such close proximity—the victims in anonymity, the victimizer glorified.[122] This disputed 'heritage of violence' raised such controversy that three members of the Commission refused to endorse the recommendation of the removal of the bodies.[123] Dead bodies, due to their effectiveness as 'political symbol',[124] can play an essential role in political transformations, but the relocation of bodies can also send 'disturbing signals' to the 'potential political victims' of their 'symbolic uses'.[125] The importance of the Valley as a mass grave, but also as the resting place of Franco, certainly accounts for much of the dissonance and the controversies surrounding the site.

Despite the raging controversies, the basilica was reopened to the public in December 2010, and after the change of government in 2011, the centre-right Partido Popular decided to reopen the entire Valley in June 2012, except for the base of the cross while under construction. The accession to power in 2011 of the Partido Popular combined with the ongoing global recession and economic crisis have not only led to funding cuts for the excavations of mass graves, but have also inhibited an expansion of Spain's memory-scape. To this day there are no plans to open an information centre or a museum at Cuelgamuros, or to transfer the remains of its two most prominent inhabitants, despite the Commission's recommendations. Further developments have followed since; in the wake of the Argentinian court case followed the United Nations' demand for

climbing the highest scaffolds and so on. Due to the lack of safety measures, many accidents occurred. It is unknown how many of these were fatal. Fernando Olmeda, *El Valle de los Caídos: una memoria de España* (Barcelona: Península, 2009), pp. 76–77. For more information on the topic of forced labour, see Fernando Mendiola Gonzalo, 'Forced labour in Franco's Spain: workforce supply, profits and productivity', Working Paper, European Historical Economics Society, 26 January 2011, pp. 1–29, available at: http://ehes.org/EHES_No4.pdf (retrieved 22 February 2012); Isaías Lafuente, *Esclavos por la patria: la explotación de los presos bajo el franquismo* (Madrid: Temas de Hoy, 2002); Gonzalo Acosta Bono, *El canal de los presos (1940–1962): trabajos forzados: de la represión política a la explotación económica* (Barcelona: Crítica, 2004).

23 The clandestine transferrals of Republican remains to the Valley of the Fallen were uncovered as recently as 2003, when a group of relatives dug up a mass grave in Aldeaseca. For a complete account, see Francisco Ferrándiz, 'Guerras sin fin: guía para descifrar el Valle de los Caídos en la España contemporánea', *Política y Sociedad*, Vol. 48, No. 3, 2011, pp. 481–500.

24 The systematic exhumation and transferral of bodies of killed Republicans from mass graves by the Francoists evokes the attempts at destruction of evidence by Nazi forces at the end of 1944, when thousands of bodies were exhumed and their remains burned in order to erase the evidence of mass murder. The removal of Republican bodies from mass graves similarly disguised the manner of their death once they arrived at the Valley of the Fallen.

25 Fernando Mendiola Gonzalo, 'Forced labor, public policies, and business strategies during Franco's dictatorship: an interim report', *Enterprise and Society*, Vol. 14, No. 1, 2013, pp. 188–189.

26 Javier Rodrigo, 'Exploitation, fascist violence and social cleansing: a study of Franco's concentration camps from a comparative perspective', *European Review of History*, Vol. 19, No. 4, 2012, p. 556.

27 The Francoists adopted a religious narrative in line with the fifteenth-century *Reconquista* campaign against the Moors by the Catholic Monarchs and placed the Republicans in the role of the 'anti-Spain' against which their 'Crusade' was directed. Moreover, the 'mission to purge, re-educate and exploit the nation's enemies' and its connection to traditional and Catholic values can clearly be seen in the transformatory as well as economic character of the penal system and the use of the Catholic concept of atonement or 'redemption' in the Redemption of Prison Sentences through Labour Scheme. See Rodrigo, 'Exploitation', p. 561.

28 Mendiola Gonzalo, 'Forced labor, public policies', p. 188.

29 Preston, *The Spanish holocaust*, p. 503.

30 Agencia Estatal Boletín Oficial del Estado, 'Boletín Oficial del Estado, Número 62', 1 March 1940, available at: http://www.boe.es/datos/pdfs/BOE/1940/062/A01537-01539.pdf (retrieved 23 April 2013).

31 For a more detailed account of the different forms of Republican repression under Franco, see, for example, Paloma Aguilar, *Memory and amnesia: the role of the Spanish Civil War in the transition to democracy* (New York: Berghahn Books, 2002); Michael Richards, *A time of silence: civil war and the culture of repression in Franco's Spain, 1936–1945* (Cambridge: Cambridge University Press, 2006); Francisco Agramunt Lacruz, *Arte y represión en la guerra civil española: artistas en checas, cárceles y campos de concentración* (Valencia: Generalitat Valenciana, 2005); Matilde Eiroa, 'Las fuentes doctrinales: pensamiento y lenguaje de la represión sistémica (1936–1948)', in Julio Aróstegui Sánchez (ed.), *Franco, la represión como sistema* (Barcelona: Flor del Viento, 2012), pp. 107–162.

32 Sueiro, *Verdadera*, p. 67.

33 The architect of the Valley of the Fallen, Diego Méndez, stated in 1957 that a total of only 2,000 workers had been employed in the project since the 1940s, and that only eighty of these had been political prisoners. Tomás Borrás, 'Novena maravilla: el Valle de los Caídos', *ABC*, 21 July 1957, pp. 31–34, at p. 31. Furthermore, Isaías Lafuente estimates the number of political prisoners at work in Cuelgamuros at 7,000 (Lafuente, *Esclavos por la patria*, pp. 118–119). The figure of 20,000 has been given by several renowned scholars, such as Preston, *The Spanish holocaust*, p. 659; Sueiro, *Verdadera*, p. 118; and Helen Graham, *The Spanish Civil War: a very short introduction* (Oxford: Oxford University Press, 2005), p. 131.

34 All translations in this article are my own, unless otherwise stated.

35 Juan Blanco, *Valle de los Caídos: ni presos políticos ni trabajos forzados* (Madrid: Fuerza Nueva, 2009), p. 133; Blanco, 'Valle de los Caídos: ni presos políticos, ni trabajos forzados', *Razón española: Revista bimestral de pensamiento*, Vol. 161, 2010, pp. 329–333; Pío Moa, 'El Valle de los Caídos', Generalísimo Francisco Franco, first printed in *La Razón*, 27 April 2005, available at: http://www.generalisimofranco.com/opinion/184.htm (retrieved 31 July 2014); Moa, 'Prólogo', in Pablo Linares and José María Manrique, *El Valle de los Caídos, crónica de una persecución salvaje* (Valladolid; Galland, 2011); César Alcalá, *Secretos y mentiras de los Franco* (Barcelona: Styria, 2008), pp. 301–320; Carmelo Jordá, Interview with Pablo Linares, Libertad Digital, 5 May 2010, available at: http://www.libertaddigital.com/sociedad/la-del-valle-de-los-caidos-es-la-unica-iglesia-del-mundo-cerrada-por-orden-gubernamental-1276391885/1.html (retrieved 23 August 2014).

36 Pura Sánchez Sánchez, *Individuas de dudosa moral: la represión de las mujeres en Andalucía, 1936–1958* (Barcelona: Crítica, 2009), pp. 148–149.
37 Oriol Martí, 'La Copel: historia de una lucha silenciada', *El Viejo Topo*, Vol. 13, 1977, p. 38.
38 José Manuel Sabín, *Prisión y muerte en la España de la postguerra* (Madrid: Muchnik, 1996), pp. 224–231.
39 Lafuente, *Esclavos por la patria*, pp. 61–65.
40 Acosta Bono, *El canal*, pp. 214–223; Eduardo de Guzmán, *Nosotros, los asesinos: Memorias de la guerra de España* (Madrid: Del Toro, 1976), pp. 388–389.
41 The number of only fourteen deaths stated by the political prisoner Ángel Lausín, who worked as a medical doctor at the Valley, is disputed. Sueiro, *Verdadera*, p. 76. Lausín was not present for the entire duration of the construction; he arrived at the Valley at the end of 1944. Olmeda, *El Valle de los Caídos*, pp. 76–77.
42 Olmeda, *El Valle de los Caídos*, pp. 75–76.
43 Mónica Vázquez Astorga, 'Los monumentos a los caídos: 'Un patrimonio para la memoria o para el olvido?', *Anales de Historia del Arte*, Vol. 16, 2006, p. 285.
44 It needs to be mentioned, however, that the commemoration and heroization of the war dead and in particular fallen soldiers after the end of the First World War was a common feature throughout Europe. Post-1918, war memorials to the fallen were erected throughout the countries that had participated in the First World War. For an in-depth discussion of this topic, see Jay Winter, *Sites of memory, sites of mourning: the Great War in European cultural history* (Cambridge: Cambridge University Press, 2005), in particular ch. 4; and Timothy G. Ashplant, Graham Dawson and Michael Roper, 'The politics of war memory and commemoration: contexts, structures and dynamics', in Timothy G. Ashplant, Graham Dawson and Michael Roper (eds.), *The politics of war memory and commemoration* (London: Routledge, 2000), pp. 3–86.
45 Benedict Anderson, *Imagined communities: reflections on the origin and spread of nationalism* (London: Verso, 2006), p. 6.
46 The year 1492 with the completion of the reconquest of Spain, and the so-called discovery of the Americas in the same year which established Spain as a colonial power, was regarded as the starting point of Spain's glory.
47 Eric J. Hobsbawm, 'Introduction: inventing traditions', in Eric J. Hobsbawm and Terrence Ranger (eds.), *The invention of tradition* (Cambridge: Cambridge University Press, 1983), pp. 1–14.
48 Dacia Viejo Rose, *Reconstructing Spain: cultural heritage and memory after civil war* (Brighton: Sussex Academic, 2011), p. 81.
49 Brian Graham, Gregory J. Ashworth and John E. Tunbridge, *A geography of heritage: power, culture, and economy* (Oxford: Oxford University Press, 2000), p. 78.
50 Lynn Meskell, 'Negative heritage and past mastering in archaeology', *Anthropological Quarterly*, Vol. 75, No. 3, 2002, p. 558.
51 Blanco, 'Valle de los Caídos', p. 330; Ramón Cué, *El Valle de los Caidos, reconciliación de España* (Madrid: El autor, 1976).
52 Ávalos was an unlikely choice for the sculptor of the Francoists' most important monument. He was a socialist and, unlike Méndez, had not been a supporter of Franco; he hence suffered from reprisals under the application of the LRP and went into 'voluntary' exile in Portugal between 1944 and 1950. Franco discovered Ávalos' work at an exhibition in 1950 and was convinced that he was the 'great sculptor Spain needed' for the Valley of the Fallen; Ávalos then won the subsequently announced competition to create the sculptures at the Valley. Olmeda, *El Valle de los Caídos*, pp. 160–161.
53 Sueiro, *Verdadera*, pp. 165–170.
54 Forest and Johnson, 'Unraveling', p. 530.
55 Local monuments to Francoist fallen had been erected by supportive communities prior to the November 1938 decree that stipulated the placing of names of the Francoist fallen beneath a cross affixed to a church wall. Peter Anderson, 'In the name of the martyrs: memory and retribution in Francoist southern Spain, 1936–45′, *Cultural and Social History*, Vol. 8, No. 3, 2011, p. 364. The symbolic significance of monuments to the dead was declared in the 'Manifesto of Madrid' soon after the Civil War; the 'Manifesto' also introduced the Escorial as the point of departure for the development of a national architecture. Miguel Alonso del Val, 'Spanish architecture 1939–1958: continuity and diversity', *Architectural Association School of Architecture*, Vol. 17, 1989, p. 58.
56 For more details on the basilica, the artists and their work, see Sueiro, *Verdadera*.
57 Official website of the Abbey of the Valley of the Fallen, Abadía de la Santa Cruz, 2010, available at: http://www.valledeloscaidos.es/monumento/paso (retrieved 15 February 2013).
58 Sueiro, *Verdadera*, pp. 184–185.
59 The mosaic was blackened by the smoke of a bomb that had exploded in the basilica in 1999, and only cleaned in 2009. Diego Barcala, 'Apología restaurada de Falange Española', *Público*, 3 May 2010, available at: http://www.publico.es/espana/309709/apologia-restaurada-de-falange-espanola (retrieved 2 February 2013). I am grateful to one of the reviewers of this article for pointing out its full visibility in May 2014.

60 Sueiro, *Verdadera*, pp. 140, 187; Forensic report by Dr. Andrés Bedate Gutiérrez on the feasibility of identification of remains buried in the Valley of the Fallen, 'Viabilidad de identificación en el enterramiento del Valle de los Caídos', Spanish Ministry of Justice, 3 May 2011, pp. 2–3, available at: http://www.memoriahistorica.gob.es/NR/rdonlyres/326E9950-5FDA-482A-BF15-0DE8933D49C9/153421/informeforensevalledeloscaidos.pdf (retrieved 1 February 2013).
61 Alejandro González-Varas Ibáñez, 'El Valle de los Caídos: memoria y futuro jurídico', *Jornadas derechos humanos y memoria histórica*, 13 February 2012, p. 5, available at: http://derechosociales.unizar.es/Documenta/GzVaras.pdf (retrieved 16 March 2012).
62 Pierre Bourdieu, *Language and symbolic power*, ed. John B. Thompson, trans. Gino Raymond and Matthew Adamson (Cambridge, MA: Harvard University Press, 1991), pp. 238–239.
63 The official commemoration of the uprising took place on 18 July. The uprising took place on 17–18 July 1936; 18 July was declared a national holiday in July 1937. The anniversary of the victory was also designated as such in March 1940. Paloma Aguilar and Carsten Humlebæk, 'Collective memory and national identity in the Spanish democracy', *History and Memory*, Vol. 14, No. 1, 2002, p. 124.
64 Sueiro, *Verdadera*, pp. 201–202.
65 José María Calleja, *El Valle de los Caídos* (Madrid: Espasa, 2009), p. 113.
66 Calleja, *El Valle de los Caídos*, p. 114.
67 Olmeda, *El Valle de los Caídos*, p. 200.
68 Tunbridge and Ashworth, *Dissonant heritage*, p. 102.
69 Aleida Assmann, *Cultural memory and western civilization: functions, media, archives* (Cambridge: Cambridge University Press, 2011), p. 321.
70 Queralt Solé i Barjau, 'Inhumados en el Valle de los Caídos: los primeros traslados desde la provincia de Madrid', *Hispania Nova: Revista de Historia Contemporánea*, Vol. 9, 2009, pp. 1–32, at p. 7.
71 Olmeda, *El Valle de los Caídos*, p. 157.
72 For a concise account of the shift in the official discourse, see Aguilar, *Memory and amnesia*, pp. 74–85.
73 Alcalá, *Secretos*, pp. 312–315; Moa, 'El Valle de los Caídos'.
74 Official State Gazette, 'Boletín Oficial del Estado, Número 127', 28 May 2011, available at: https://www.boe.es/boe/dias/2011/05/28/pdfs/BOE-A-2011-9320.pdf (retrieved 5 February 2013), p. 53148.
75 Calleja, *El Valle de los Caídos*, p. 117.
76 Solé i Barjau, 'Inhumados', p. 19.
77 Solé i Barjau, 'Inhumados', pp. 8, 25.
78 Olmeda, *El Valle de los Caídos*, p. 223.
79 Solé i Barjau, 'Inhumados', p. 25.
80 Solé i Barjau, 'Inhumados', p. 19; Diego Barcala, 'Mi padre está en la caja 198, en la cripta derecha', *Público*, 13 October 2010, available at: http://www.publico.es/espana/341266/mi-padre-esta-en-la-caja-198-en-la-cripta-derecha (retrieved 5 March 2012).
81 As a result of the 'Paracuellos incident', the necessity of consent from families for the transferral of bodies (which, in any case, mainly applied to non-Republican bodies) was revoked in 1960. Furthermore, the transferral became mandatory if families did not pay for the upkeep of the graves. Olmeda, *El Valle de los Caídos*, p. 265.
82 Quoted in Ferrándiz, 'Guerras sin fin', pp. 493–494.
83 Calleja, *El Valle de los Caídos*, p. 117.
84 Report on the future of the Valley of the Fallen, Ministerio de la Presidencia, 29 November 2011, pp. 1–30, at p. 3, available at: http://digital.csic.es/handle/10261/85710 (retrieved 10 November 2014).
85 Sueiro, *Verdadera*, p. 272.
86 See, for example, Alcalá, *Secretos*, p. 311.
87 Sueiro, *Verdadera*, p. 209.
88 Sueiro, *Verdadera*, p. 273.
89 José F. Colmeiro, *Memoria histórica e identidad cultural: de la postguerra a la postmodernidad* (Rubí, Barcelona: Anthropos, 2005), pp. 20–22.
90 Katherine Hite, 'The Valley of the Fallen: tales from the crypt', *Forum for Modern Language Studies*, Vol. 44, No. 2, 2008, pp. 117–118.
91 Macdonald, 'Undesirable heritage', p. 11.
92 Ulrich Winter, '"Localizar a los muertos" y "reconocer al otro"', in Joan Ramon Resina and Ulrich Winter (eds.), *Casa encantada: lugares de memoria en la España constitucional, 1978–2004* (Madrid: Iberoamericana, 2005), p. 19.
93 Winter, 'Localizar', pp. 27–28.
94 Gareth Stockey, *Valley of the Fallen: the (n)ever changing faces of General Franco's monument* (Nottingham: CCP, 2013), pp. 30–31, 72–85.

95 Aguilar, *Memory and amnesia*, pp. 74–85; Paloma Aguilar, 'Los lugares de la memoria de la Guerra civil. El Valle de los Caídos, la ambigüedad calculada', in Javier Tusell (ed.), *El régimen de Franco (1936–1975)*, 2 Vols. (Madrid: UNED, 1993), 1: pp. 485–498.
96 Stockey, *Valley of the Fallen*, pp. 9–28.
97 Stockey, *Valley of the Fallen*, p. 50.
98 Stockey, *Valley of the Fallen*, pp. 10–11, 17, 20–21, 73.
99 Stockey, *Valley of the Fallen*, pp. 63–64.
100 Proshansky, 'The city and self-identity', p. 155.
101 Maurice Halbwachs, *The collective memory*, trans. Francis J. Ditter and Vida Yazdi Ditter (New York: Harper, 1980), p. 130.
102 Winter, 'Localizar', pp. 19–20.
103 Sharon MacDonald, 'Words in stone? Agency and identity in a Nazi landscape', *Journal of Material Culture*, Vol. 11, No. 1, 2006, p. 106.
104 Aguilar and Humlebæk, 'Collective memory', pp. 128–129.
105 Aguilar and Humlebæk, 'Collective memory', pp. 128–129.
106 Official State Gazette, 'Boletín Oficial del Estado, Número 310', 27 December 2007, pp. 53411–53415, available at: http://www.boe.es/boe/dias/2007/12/27/pdfs/A53410-53416.pdf (retrieved 23 July 2010).
107 The pre-constitutional coat of arms with the imperial eagle can be found carved in stone at both ends of the arches delimiting the exedra of the basilica, as well as engraved in stone and on various pieces of the furniture and the choir of the main altar. The crest sometimes also appears in simplified form. Spanish Government website, 'Balance general de retirada de vestigios de la Administración General del Estado', Gobierno de España, July 2011, p. 18, available at: http://www.memoriahistorica.gob.es/NR/rdonlyres/225254CC-7460-4875-B15C-25D9F5B3ED09/179746/BDVestigiosMHjulio2011.pdf (retrieved 3 August 2014).
108 Katherine Hite, *Politics and the art of commemoration: memorials to struggle in Latin America and Spain* (New York: Routledge, 2011), p. 26.
109 Blanco, 'Valle de los Caídos', p. 330.
110 Forest and Johnson, 'Unraveling', pp. 525–527.
111 Forest and Johnson, 'Unraveling', p. 525.
112 The scope of this article does not allow for an in-depth discussion of the Garzón case and its wide-ranging implications. See Giles Tremlett, 'Baltasar Garzón cleared over his Franco-era crimes inquiry', *Guardian*, 27 February 2012, available at: http://www.theguardian.com/world/2012/feb/27/baltasar-garzon-cleared-franco-crimes (retrieved 2 July 2012). For details concerning the Valley, see Ferrándiz, 'Guerras sin fin'.
113 Luciana Bertoia, 'Franco-era officials get closer to extradition', *Buenos Aires Herald*, 30 November 2013, available at: http://www.buenosairesherald.com/article/146350/francoera-officials-get-closer-to-extradition (retrieved 8 January 2013).
114 Hirsch, 'The generation of postmemory', p. 106.
115 Marianne Hirsch, 'Surviving images: Holocaust photographs and the work of postmemory', *Yale Journal of Criticism*, Vol. 14, No. 1, 2001, p. 12.
116 Ferrándiz, 'Guerras sin fin', pp. 491–492.
117 Bedate Gutiérrez, 'Viabilidad', pp. 2–7.
118 Quoted in Ferrándiz, 'Guerras sin fin', p. 495.
119 Calleja, *El Valle de los Caídos*, p. 112.
120 Report on the future of the Valley of the Fallen, p. 7.
121 '"Dignidad democrática" o "cuestión histórica": 'debería Franco ser exhumado?', 20minutos.es, 30 October 2013, available at: http://www.20minutos.es/noticia/1962769/0/argumentos/exhumacion/franco-valle-de-los-caidos/ (retrieved 20 August 2014).
122 'Franco's tomb divides Spain decades after death', *Japantimes*, 21 November, 2013, available at: http://www.japantimes.co.jp/news/2013/11/21/world/politics-diplomacy-world/francos-tomb-divides-spain-decades-after-death/#.U__YFGccSM8 (retrieved 29 August 2014).
123 Stockey, *Valley of the Fallen*, p. 87.
124 Katherine Verdery. *The political lives of dead bodies: Reburial and postsocialist change* (New York: Columbia University Press, 1999), p. 33.
125 Tunbridge and Ashworth, *Dissonant heritage*, p. 53.
126 James Mayo, 'War memorials as political memory', *Geographical Review*, Vol. 78, No. 1, 1988, p. 67.
127 Vinyes, 'La reconciliación'.
128 Alex Boraine, *A country unmasked: South Africa's truth and reconciliation commission* (Capetown: Oxford University Press, 2001), p. 20.
129 Nora, 'Between memory and history', p. 12.

Holocaust commemoration in Romania: Roma and the contested politics of memory and memorialization

MICHELLE KELSO and DAINA S. EGLITIS

In 2009, the Romanian government unveiled a $7.4 million Holocaust memorial to commemorate over 280,000 Jews and 11,000 Roma who died as victims of the Ion Antonescu regime. Located in central Bucharest, the monument is part of a national agenda, outlined by an international commission, to study the crimes of the Holocaust in Romania and to help the country come to terms with historical atrocities. Under communism and in the early post-communist period, the Romanian state denied its role in the Holocaust. In this article, we explore the representation of the Holocaust and, in particular, Roma victims in the dominant historical narrative and the Holocaust memorial. We delve into discourses around this monument, which feed into a larger dialogue of victim recognition and contested national narratives about the Holocaust. We highlight the construction and contestation of the Holocaust memorial, considering in particular the paradox of Roma victims and suggesting that Roma are simultaneously *represented*, *unrepresented* and *misrepresented* in the historical story and memorial of the Holocaust in Romania.

Introduction

When the regime of General Ion Antonescu (1940–44) undertook the meticulously planned deportation of Romanian Roma, Dumitru Trancă was just seven years old. Trancă's parents, ethnic Roma coppersmiths, travelled with their five children in a horse-drawn caravan, selling pots and tools to Romanian peasants. Unbeknownst to them, Romanian authorities had labelled certain 'Gypsies' threats to national purity and security. Rural police deported the Trancă family and over 25,000 other Roma to concentration camps in Romanian-occupied Ukraine, where forced labour, disease, exposure and starvation brought mass suffering and death. Trancă's two youngest sisters wasted away from typhus before the camps were liberated by Soviet troops in 1944. In October 2009, sixty-seven years after he was deported, Trancă was invited to speak at the unveiling of a $7.4 million Holocaust memorial to commemorate Jewish and Roma victims of the Holocaust.

The monument, which stands in central Bucharest, has generated contestation and controversy. Many advocates of the monument's construction, including Holocaust survivor and Nobel Prize winner Elie Wiesel, were adamant that it should function to honour victims and educate future generations.[1] Some Romanian political leaders envisioned the monument as a portal into the past, a marker that would enlighten the public about the historical silences imposed by earlier regimes. President Traian Băsescu suggested at the opening ceremony that the monument 'confirms Romania's decision to recover its real history. It is a difficult process that means changing mentalities and the capacity to accept reality after 50–60 years when history was falsified'.[2]

While Roma victims like Dumitru Trancă and his family are represented in the memorial, their experiences of the atrocities remain underrepresented in Holocaust literature and their voices have been marginal in the construction of a contemporary national narrative of the past in Romania. As this article will show, their representation in the memorial is itself something of a paradox, as it both illuminates and obscures their historical voices and experiences.

From the vast expanse of events that comprise the history of territories and their inhabitants, a national history is constructed by powerful actors who select the 'mentions' and 'silences' that will become the dominant narrative of the past.[3] Access to the power to define the parameters of the dominant historical narrative is uneven. In the communist period, the authoritarian state drew the outlines of acceptable historical memory through texts, political manifestos, cultural products and commemorative practices that carefully controlled the remembrance of actors and events of the past. The dominant historical narrative served the needs of communist central authority and ideology, conferring legitimacy on the power of the state and party.[4] Coercive measures relegated counter-hegemonic narratives of the past to the margins of social remembering and individual or community memory became the repository of alternative historical stories.

In the post-communist period, communist institutions, ideology and dominant narratives of the past have largely been swept away. New sets of actors have emerged in the region of East Central Europe to contribute to and contest the construction of a hegemonic narrative that will represent a 'normal' past. Jeffrey Olick suggests that societies produce 'ideas of what a normal past should look like, and [use] those images as ideals to strive for or denied rights to long for'. Indeed, post-communist states and societies across the region have engaged in politics of memory that elevate selected events and heroes, while casting actors and experiences that fail to fit the political and social needs of the present into the shadows.[5] The treatment of the Holocaust in post-communist national historical narratives in East and Central European countries in particular suggests a selective use of the past to highlight victimization of the titular nation: the emphasis in post-communist memorialization of the past has been on the crimes of communism. As historian James Mark points out, modern memorials at sites of terror are commemorations of individual suffering, but also portray communist nations as victims. He adds, however, that these memorials function in the production of a 'selective authenticity' that downplays national complicity in wartime crimes, including the

Holocaust, and mutes discussion of the suffering of minority groups.[6] In Romania, this process of producing a 'normal' history has been further complicated by contestation over Romania's communist past.[7]

The concept of collective memory is largely grounded in the work of sociologist Maurice Halbwachs, who posits that memory is socially determined. That is, memory is the product of social communication and interaction. Collective memory imbues the past with meaning and contributes to the collective identity of social groups. History—or the dominant narrative of history—is thus a social construction rooted in the needs, interests, beliefs and aspirations of the present.[8] Arguably, the Halbwachian conception of collective memory under-theorizes the role of power in the construction and reconstruction of dominant historical narratives. Richard Lebow highlights this dimension, utilizing the term 'institutional memory', which he defines as 'efforts by political elites, their supporters, and their opponents to construct meanings of the past and propagate them more widely or impose them on other members of society'.[9]

In this article, following the work of sociologist Pierre Bourdieu, we envision the politics of memory in Romania as a *field*, that is, a system of social positions structured by power relations.[10] Agents in the field bring differing forms and amounts of capital to the field, where they seek to trade capital for the power to define dominant narratives of memory (what Lebow terms institutional memory). What is at stake is the power to 'achieve hegemony for their preferred memory'[11]—that is, to mark the parameters of history, heroes, villains, victims and the social hierarchies that underpin political legitimacy and social position. By conceptualizing the dominant narrative of the past as a field, we seek to recognize the contestation surrounding the representation and memorialization of the Holocaust and, in particular, the experiences of Romanian Roma in the Holocaust. We follow Bourdieu in his key assumption that capital, and the power it confers, is not equitably distributed in society. As such, the politics of the past are fundamentally contentious and are structured by struggles between actors with divergent interests and diverse stores of capital to trade for historical representation.

This article endeavours to develop a historical overview of the Romanian Roma experience of the Holocaust and to examine the representation of that experience in the post-war and post-communist periods, with a particular focus on the memorialization of victims of the Romanian Holocaust on the monument unveiled in Bucharest in 2009. Among the questions raised by this article are the following: How did Romanian Roma experience the Holocaust? How were their experiences represented in the post-war communist period? How have they been represented and commemorated in post-communist Romania? Who are the key actors in the field of Holocaust memory and its commemoration in post-communist Romania? Why have Roma been marginal in the key narratives of Romania's past and how is this reflected in Bucharest's memorial?

In answering these questions, we make use of both primary and secondary sources available in Romanian, Romani and English. Our primary data set for this project is ethnographic and archival research. From 2004 to 2006, one of the authors, Michelle Kelso, was based in Bucharest, where she spent twenty-two months interviewing Romani Holocaust survivors. Roma recounted their experiences of deportation, deprivation, disease and the death of loved ones. They offered family and community oral histories. Few of these stories have been published.[12] Our work also draws on observations of the process of and debates over the construction of the Holocaust memorial in Bucharest, including interviews and press accounts. The article makes use of archival data that highlights the targeting and treatment of the Roma in World War II, as well as their return at the conclusion of the conflict. Secondary literature is used to develop a framework for understanding the politics of representation in the communist and post-communist periods in Romania and to offer a systematic examination of the key actors in the field of Holocaust memory politics and memorialization.

The case of Roma and the Holocaust in Romania

The pro-fascist regime of Antonescu implemented a campaign of deportation and murder against Romania's Jews and Roma.[13] Antonescu came to power after King Carol II abdicated in 1940, first in a joint leadership with the Iron Guard party and then as an authoritarian ruler after January 1941. Antonescu harboured a strong suspicion of Jews, as well as ideas of ethnic purity that mirrored those embraced by his Nazi allies. The destruction of Romanian Jews and Roma was part of a broader bio-political goal to 'return' the country to ethnic purity through 'Romanianization'.[14] The Antonescu regime designed and implemented plans to cleanse Romania of its 'undesirable' minorities. After 'ethnic purification' had begun with Jewish victims mainly from the regions of Bessarabia and Bukovina, the Romanian regime turned its attention to parts of the Romani community.

Romania joined the war on 22 June 1941, participating in Hitler's planned invasion of the Soviet Union. Confident of victory, Antonescu had formed a plan for the Jews in the northern and eastern provinces. When the attack on the USSR was underway, Antonescu ordered mass killings of Jews in Bessarabia and Bukovina in a 'cleansing the land' campaign that the army and the gendarmerie carried out during the summer of 1941.[15] In the initial phase of the genocide, between 45,000 and 60,000 Jews were killed.[16] Those Jews who survived were pushed into Transnistria, an area between the Rivers Dniester and Bug that came under Romanian control in August 1941.[17] Antonescu agreed to a Romanian administration of Transnistria, an agricultural region with less than half of the population of Romanian descent, in exchange for economic exploitation of the region throughout the war. Once in possession of Transnistria, Romania deported over 150,000 Jews there. Transnistria was also to be the final destination of thousands of deported Roma.

A year after launching brutal attacks on the country's Jews, the Antonescu regime turned its attention to the Roma. Most *ţigani* (translated as Gypsies) were rural inhabitants, working as unskilled labourers in agriculture or as craftsmen. Since their emancipation from 500 years of slavery in 1855–56, the process of integration had been painfully slow. Roma remained a poor, illiterate and marginalized minority group.[18] Antonescu ordered several surveys in 1942 to assess the number and residency of *ţigani*, and statisticians at the Central Institute for Statistics estimated in their report that, taking into account territorial losses from the war, the Gypsy population was around 208,700.[19]

The Roma issue remained fairly marginal in public discourse, most likely due to their low socio-economic status, whereas the preoccupation with the 'Jewish problem' remained prominent. For nomads, there was no indication that they would be targeted by the regime as the first Romani group for deportation to Transnistria.[20] They were the least integrated in society, therefore less likely to inter-marry with Romanians and a lesser threat to the Romanian nation, according to the regime's standards. At the same time, it is possible that they were targeted first as a weaker group whose deportation would raise minimum opposition. While previous governments had targeted Jews through legislation, Roma experienced no change in their status as citizens, though life became harder for nomadic groups after legislation passed in 1940 that restricted the movement of nomads over fears that they could spread disease. Then, in early 1942, Antonescu identified criteria that would later be used as the basis for deportation: all Gypsies living a nomadic lifestyle and settled Gypsies who were considered to be 'dangerous'—those holding criminal convictions and those without regular forms of employment—were potential targets.[21]

Shortly afterwards, deportation orders imposed a sweep of nomads, who were to be expelled and placed in camps in Transnistria. Antonescu ordered the General Inspectorate of the Gendarmerie (IGJ) to supervise the deportation of nomadic Roma whose caravans would serve as their transportation across the border. By the end of August 1942, officials estimated that 11,441 nomadic *ţigani* had crossed into Transnistria.[22]

Gendarmes in Transnistria assigned the Roma to localities mainly along the Bug River. The former Prefect of Oceacov wrote in his memoir of the arrival of the nomads:

> During one week 15,000 [sic] Gypsies arrived. The commander of the gendarmes reported to me verbally ... that [the Gypsies] were in an incredible state of misery ... there were a lot of old people, women, and children. In the wagons there were paralyzed, older persons well over 70 years of age, blind and on the verge of death. The great majority of them were naked in rags ... They protested, they screamed, they cried, they ranted: why were we arrested and sent to Transnistria?[23]

In September 1942, deportations of settled *ţigani* began. In May, the Interior Ministry had ordered the police to conduct a census of *ţigani* considered dangerous to the regime—those with criminal records and without stable employment. Some 31,438 *ţigani* matched the Ministry's criteria for deportation.[24] Just over 12,000 of those Roma considered by authorities as the most dangerous, undesirable and unfit for military service were destined for the first train transport. The remaining 18,262 *ţigani*, as calculated by the Ministry, were to be deported early in 1943.[25]

Roma suffering in Transnistria was acute.[26] Transnistrian camps such as Bogdanovka and Dumanovka, sites of major massacres of Jews, were also sites of death and destruction of Roma. Historian Viorel Achim writes that 'the situation of the Gypsies cannot be thought of much differently than the intent in that moment for the Jewish population, which earlier had meant the end for many deportees'.[27] During the winter of 1942–43, typhus killed thousands as it spread quickly among Roma housed in overcrowded schools, houses, barracks and shacks. Starvation killed thousands more as Romanian authorities sporadically delivered food rations, reducing deportees to walking skeletons.[28] Survivor Ion Neagu remembered that sometimes parents sent their children to procure food, and they didn't always return: 'I remember when three or four children left—seven, eight and ten years old—to get potatoes from the field. Only one of them came back. Shot. A bullet went through his back and came out his chest'.[29]

In the early months of 1944, the Soviet army mounted an offensive to recapture its occupied territory and Axis troops retreated. This meant that liberation of Jews and Roma who were left alive in camps effectively occurred through abandonment by their guards. On 23 August 1944, King Mihai announced the dissolution of the Antonescu government and proclaimed an armistice with the Allies. Upon their arrival home, many Roma succumbed to untreated illnesses such as typhus and tuberculosis. The majority discovered that there was nothing left of their pre-war possessions. Roma survivors had few opportunities to give public voice to their traumatic experiences. They strove to settle back into some semblance of their pre-war life, which was difficult as the country transitioned rapidly from fascism to communism. While some survivors recall having told their non-Roma neighbours of their experiences, they also attempted to blend into the post-war population to avoid being targeted again for their skin colour and cultural practices by 'Romanianizing' as much as possible.

Survivor Ion Cioaba, a Romani leader who in 1992 self-coronated as the 'International King of the Gypsies', convinced many Roma to forgo their nomadic roots and adopt a Romanianized lifestyle.[30] His wife Lucia Mihai recounted that Cioaba, affected by his Transnistrian experiences, sought conformity as a means of countering future persecutions. He gave up their horse wagon, built a house, put their children in school and cut his traditional waist-length hair, going against their cultural norms. She remembered him telling others:

> I want everyone to see this—for all of us to be like one another, as the Romanians do, as people are, for us to be like people, too ... Be careful, behave, because you heard about the tragedy in Transnistria ... So that should never happen again. Who knows who might find you—you could be like before and frighten them. And now look. We are all gentlemen. You all have houses, cars, everything.[31]

Clearly, Roma persecution under the Antonescu regime was ferocious. Yet it has been marginal, as we will show, to dominant narratives of the Holocaust in both the post-war and post-communist periods.

Post-war history: history and the Holocaust in communist Romania

Upon liberation in 1944, fewer than half of the 25,000 Roma deported at the start of the war had survived.[32] Notably as well, their experiences were largely consigned to the silences of World War II history. Romanian communist leaders and historians, labelled 'history cleansers' by historian Randolph Braham, transformed the Holocaust into a Nazi-centred story, denying the existence and crimes of Romanian genocidaires and obscuring the ethnicity of their victims.[33] As James Mark notes, 'although [communists] placed Fascism at the centre of their commemorative tradition, they referred to the suffering of the nation, or of the working class under Fascism, but beyond that seldom focused on a particular ethnic or religious group'.[34]

The post-war Soviet narrative had a powerful influence in Romania, which, like many of its communist neighbours, acted to shape public memory of World War II and the Holocaust in a manner that elevated national and Red Army heroism while blaming Nazi Germany for Holocaust atrocities. Communist regimes had built legitimacy in part on the foundation of anti-fascism, remembering wartime atrocities selectively. The Romanian case mirrored that of the region in many respects. Sociologist Alexandru Florian writes that under communism, 'everything Romanian was good, while the origin of evil was always from the outside'.[35] The communist state monopolized the production of the dominant historical narrative, becoming the only agent in a publicly uncontested field. While alternative narratives existed, they occupied micro-level spaces such as families and communities; individual-level memories that challenged the dominant narrative of the past were unwelcome in a public space that would not accommodate dissent or challenge.

As noted above, the state was the key agent in the production of knowledge: it exercised power through, for instance, intellectuals sympathetic to or co-opted by the Romanian communist government. Intellectuals occupied important positions in the construction of knowledge. A key vehicle for the transmission of these discourses was public education, tightly controlled by the state. For instance, state-issued textbooks mentioned victims of the Antonescu regime, but they were categorized as communists and/or Romanians rather than being identified specifically as Jews or Roma.[36]

The legitimate representation of the production of the past was carefully controlled in the latter decades of communism as well. Anthropologist Katherine Verdery writes that under Nicolae Ceaușescu, historians were referred to in the military sense as 'the historians' front', and were 'vital to shaping both the national and materialist facets of his regime's ideology and to socializing the public into a particular set of values'.[37] This required tightening central control over historiographical production. Some communist-era texts exculpated the Antonescu regime outright, projecting a dominant discourse of Romanian exceptionalism.[38] One book asserted:

> The Holocaust did not occur in Romania precisely because—with few and rather significant exceptions—the swastika-wearing executioners not only did not enjoy self-volunteered local cooperation, but also encountered outright refusal when they attempted—officially and otherwise—to recruit accomplices in the organization of the deportations or other genocidal actions.[39]

Approved published histories suggested that Romania sheltered Jews from other countries and did not serve as a site of ghettos, concentration camps or deportations to Auschwitz or Majdanek.[40] Denialism, importantly, has not only been characteristic of the communist era in Romania. Indeed, the selective 'mentions' and 'silences' of mid-twentieth-century history continued after 1989 as well.

Post-communist history: remembering and writing the Holocaust after 1989

Across the Central and Eastern European space, memorialization of the Holocaust has largely taken a position of secondary importance, behind remembrances of the nations and families who were victims of communism. Mark writes that after the fall of communism, it was not evident 'that the new political system should address the horrors of the Fascist era as well as those of the Communist'.[41] Not only were the communist-era experience and its traumas more temporally immediate, but communist governments and educational institutions had, seemingly, already plumbed the fascist era and its threats throughout the post-war period.

In Romania, the revival of Antonescu flourished after 1989, and over the next decade cemented the Holocaust exceptionalism promoted by the previous regime. Antonescu was billed as a hero for fighting communism. Foundations were established in his name, streets were renamed after him, and statues of the General were erected in several cities. As Romania consolidated its democracy and moved to join the North Atlantic Treaty Organization (NATO) and the European Union, legislative measures that forbade the promotion of fascism and Holocaust denial slowed the dissemination of the heroic image of Antonescu.[42] More rigorous scholarship on the Antonescu period occurred and Holocaust history was introduced into school curricula. Despite these measures, Antonescu remained popular. In 2006, Romanian public television sought viewer votes on the ten most popular Romanians of all times. Antonescu placed sixth,[43] coming in alongside such cultural icons as musician George Enescu, philosopher Mircea Eliade, sculptor Constantin Brancusi and gymnast Nadia Comăneci.

Decades of omission and denial have, arguably, had a persisting effect on Romanians' perceptions of the past. According to a 2010 survey, the majority of Romanians believed that the Nazis were responsible for the Holocaust in Romania, and few held Antonescu responsible for the crimes against Jews (twenty-five per cent) and Roma (thirty per cent).[44] On Romania's problematic Holocaust moral front, literary scholar Dominica Radulescu writes:

> Today, try asking a Romanian in the street ... what happened to the Jewish population of Romania between roughly 1941 and 1944. Most likely, he or she will tell you that Romania was a 'haven for Jews', that Romanians were actually good to the Jews ... Some might still tell you that Marshal Antonescu was a 'hero', a 'patriot'; others might even shock you by saying he did well to 'rid' the country of many of the Gypsies and Jews.[45]

The veneration of Antonescu has not been an ill fit with the post-communist historical turn in the region.

The post-communist construction of a Holocaust-era narrative of history has been complex and contested. Early post-communist leaders continued, with few concessions, to avoid engagement with issues of the Holocaust until 2003, when some key government officials denied publicly that the Holocaust had occurred in Romania.[46] Invited to respond to a Romanian government declaration that 'within the borders of Romania between 1940 and 1945 there was no Holocaust', then-president Ion Iliescu answered that '[t]he Holocaust was not unique to the Jewish population in Europe' and that it was 'impossible to accuse the Romanian people and the Romanian society of this [massacre of Jews]'.[47]

The 2003 incident evoked international condemnation, potentially putting at risk the country's membership in international institutions, and forced Romania to reassess its institutional memory of the Holocaust. In many post-communist states, the mantle of victimhood was embraced as exclusive rather than inclusive: in an examination of Baltic occupation museums, Aro Velmet suggests that in Estonia, for instance, the particular approach to victim status 'excludes the possible presence of other victims, or worse yet, the possibility of seeing Estonians as perpetrators of oppression'.[48] This case mirrors regional cases like Romania's: the key institutional memory about Romania and the Holocaust in the period leading up to the 2003 incident characterized the Holocaust as something that was done *to* the Romanian people, rather than something in which many Romanians, including the widely venerated Antonescu regime, were actively or passively complicit.

In response to global pressures, Iliescu created a commission composed of local and international actors to prepare an authoritative and decisive historical report. Elie Wiesel chaired the commission, having previously chaired America's President's Commission on the Holocaust, which recommended and oversaw the creation of the United States Holocaust Memorial Museum (USHMM) in Washington, DC.[49] Instead of reinforcing the dominant narrative that Romanians were victims of World War II, the commission concluded that the Romanian regime actively targeted, deported and murdered Jews and Roma.[50] Even though the report produced relatively little new knowledge,[51] it offered a fundamental challenge to the narrative.

The commission issued a spectrum of further recommendations to increase the recognition of the Holocaust as it played out in Romania, indicating that authorities should disseminate accurate historical materials on the Holocaust and organize public events and decree a national day of commemoration to raise awareness.[52] In addition, the panel recommended constructing a national memorial to the victims of the Holocaust in Romania. In the following section, we examine in greater detail the contestation and memorialization processes in Romania.

The field of modern memorialization in Romania: memory, power and history

The relationship between power and the production of knowledge is essential to understanding the formation of narratives. As James Young has argued, the meaning of the Holocaust changes according to the dominant narrative present in societies.[53] Examining Holocaust memorialization as a field in Bourdieu's sense offers the opportunity to conceptualize the power struggle surrounding the shape of the past.[54] Bourdieu conceives of a field as analogous to a game in which various actors, deploying differing stores of contextually valued capital, seek to trade their capital for that which is at stake in the field—most often power. In the case at hand, we look at power and the production of a dominant narrative of the past, highlighting key agents in the field, including Romanians espousing a perspective of Holocaust that minimalizes Romanian complicity in Holocaust crimes (a category into which many bureaucrats, teachers and others fall), Romanians trying to change this narrative to align with that of Western actors (politicians, ethnic and religious leaders, scholars, etc.) and foreign actors advocating for acceptance of a more globalized Holocaust narrative. In this section, we discuss each of these actors and the capital they bring in turn.

Among those who have resisted the dramatic changes in Romania's longtime historical narrative have been nationalist historians who occupied key positions of power under communism and, in many instances, held onto them in the post-communist period in some universities and archives,[55] as well as teachers, politicians and functionaries.[56] This category of actors brings to the field a substantial store of cultural capital, as well as a substantial degree of local control over bureaucratic structures, including those that oversee educational institutions, which might be considered a form of social capital, though it is deployed in bureaucratic structures rather than solely in social networks. A key part of contemporary civic education occurs in the classroom. School texts, written by historians and used in classrooms by history teachers, reflect primarily a nationalistic perspective that minimalizes the Holocaust, continuing for the most part the communist constructed narrative.[57] At stake for these actors is not only, in many cases, a lifetime of teaching a now-discredited story of the past, but, arguably, a national identity built in part on the very same story.

Following a regional trend of 'construct[ing] politically appropriate memories of Fascism',[58] some national actors have also pursued and embraced the post-Wiesel Commission narrative of Romanian history. Among them are prominent political leaders such as President Băsescu, former Prime Ministers Popescu-Tăriceanu and Mihai Răzvan Ungureanu, and former Foreign Minister Adrian Cioroianu, as well as cultural and academic figures and journalists. These actors bring to the field substantial stores of cultural and social capital, representing an important segment of Romania's political and intellectual elites. At stake for this group is not only the recognition of forgotten victims and the fuller articulation of Holocaust crimes, but also the opportunity to integrate the country into European structures and themselves into a globally acknowledged category of transnational actors who are key carriers of a Holocaust narrative that offers definitions of the categories of victim and perpetrator that are far more broad than those articulated in the post-war and early post-communist Romanian narratives.

Transnational actors are an important category in this field, and include those coming from foreign government institutions like the US Department of State, which is home to an office for Holocaust affairs, and the Israeli Foreign Ministry, as well as academic networks of historians and genocide scholars and cultural institutions like the USHMM and Yad Vashem. Transnational actors have, indeed, been powerfully influential across the post-communist space in asserting the need to mark Holocaust history and atrocity. According to the USHMM's website, '[t]he Museum led the international outcry and played a leading role in discussions that led Iliescu to appoint an independent commission', and one of its directors, Romanian-born Radu Ioanid, was the vice-president of the commission.[59] The insistence on fully integrating Holocaust remembrance into institutional memories of post-communist states and societies was not just symbolic: membership in key economic, political and military organizations like the EU and NATO was potentially at stake in the narrative 'return to Europe' supported by transnational actors. When the 2003 Holocaust denial went public internationally, then-Foreign Minister Mircea Geoana reacted in a letter that indicated the government's willingness to research Jewish persecutions (with no mention of Roma) as it was 'our desire to foster cooperation with the international institutions and organizations interested in this issue and with which we have always had an open dialogue'.[60]

Actors in this category come to the field of memory politics well equipped with social and cultural as well as economic capital, which is deployed to further the goal of constructing a narrative of history that comports with the global narrative. Economic capital functions here in a multitude of ways: actors like the USHMM deploy capital to mobilize and support projects like the Holocaust memorial and to expand scholarship on areas like Romani studies. Some European organizations have also funded educational initiatives on Roma, as well as the Holocaust more generally. The Council of Europe, for instance, has invested in teacher training and pedagogical materials on Romani history.[61] Arguably, this category of actors is the only one that brings substantial economic capital to the field, which underpins significant power and reach. Some, like the EU and US Department of State, are also carriers of critical political capital and they function as gatekeepers to membership in international organizations of consequence and, to some degree, access to a higher level of global prestige.

At the same time, the centrality of transnational actors in the Holocaust memorial process in Romania has been complicated. On the one hand, transnational actors like the USHMM have been instrumental in challenging exclusive entrenched historical narratives; on the other hand, their participation in the process of historical construction and memorialization has been viewed with suspicion by some groups, particularly (though not exclusively) nationalists. At a 2001 ceremony marking the Iasi pogrom, President Iliescu, arguably seeking to balance the interests of nationalists and the pursuit of Romanian membership in NATO, declared that, 'no matter what we may think, international public opinion considers Antonescu to have been a war criminal'.[62] His comments, though hardly iconoclastic, provoked a local political backlash.[63]

Romani survivors have been conspicuously absent as actors in the field of memory politics in Romania. However, young Roma activists are becoming increasingly significant in the field of commemoration. Florin Manole, Romani activist and elected city councilman, lobbies for Romani representation in Holocaust-related legislation and events. In 2007, President Băsescu decorated some

Jewish Holocaust survivors with medals of honour on Romania's Holocaust Remembrance Day. Manole, in attendance, discovered that no Roma survivors had been invited to receive medals. On site he called one of Băsescu's advisors and gave him an ultimatum: fix the oversight within two hours or face a press scandal for discrimination.[64] Within two weeks, a separate ceremony was held for three Romani survivors. Marian Mandache, director of one of the largest Roma non-governmental organizations (NGOs) in Romania, suggests that Romani commemoration has lagged because, amid the plethora of human rights issues currently facing Roma and NGOs advocating on their behalf, there is a dearth of time, personnel or funds to take on the effort of educating Romanians about Roma Holocaust history: 'I am working to keep Roma from being evicted from their houses, and follow cases of discrimination against Roma. There are so many social issues and too few of us to do the work'.[65]

A spectrum of actors has struggled to incorporate competing visions of the past into historical education, cultural representation and commemorations.[66] The decision by the Romanian leadership to embrace a transformed narrative of the past and to embody that narrative in the form of a Holocaust memorial in Bucharest suggests that the 'winners' in the field of memory politics are those actors who have embraced a more globalized and inclusive narrative and who have pursued a reconstructed narrative of the past that recasts Romanians into more complex roles and expands the recognition of victims. At the same time, questions remain about the full representation of groups like the Roma in the dominant memory narrative.

Building history: the Holocaust memorial in Bucharest

Bucharest's Holocaust memorial, located in the city centre, is approachable from all sides, occupying a square city block flanked by parked cars. Rust-coloured metal sheets demarcate the edge of the park and the memorial, giving the appearance of an unfinished building site. The entrance of the memorial site opens onto a parking lot behind which heavy traffic moves along the banks of the Dambovita Canal. Six key elements are incorporated in the monument: a seven-metre high column of remembrance, Via Dolorosa (a symbol of train tracks), a central memorial building, the Epitaph (a sculpture symbolizing a mass grave), the Star of David (a sculpture of the Jewish symbol) and a wagon wheel (a sculpture of the Romani symbol). The memorial is, in a sense, a monument to the efforts of both national and transnational actors to construct a new narrative of the Holocaust past and to embody it in a structure that is central and striking.

Unveiled in 2009, the memorial encountered a spectrum of obstacles on its way to completion, which included not only historical representation of victims, but also political and environmental conflicts. In 2006, the Romanian Ministry of Culture (MCC), the central government institution tasked with administering the Holocaust memorial, chose a site in a small public park located across from the Ministry of the Interior, whose gendarmes and police had carried out Antonescu's deportations of Jews and Roma during the war. The district mayor's office ceded the green space. Controversy erupted soon thereafter around the memorial's proposed location. Two groups—city officials and conservationists—opposed the site choice for different reasons, delaying its construction.

The historical representation of victim groups in the memorial was a negotiated process, with discussions around not only how victims would be represented, but which ones would be included in the memorial. Virgil Nitulescu, then-Director of Administration at the MCC, headed a committee composed of artists, Jewish survivors, historians and former Wiesel commissioners to select the memorial design. In 2006, Romanian-born German sculptor Peter Jacobi won the monument competition. Jacobi recounted in an interview that the final memorial was a compromise between his vision and the desires of the Jewish community to see 'blood expressionism'.[67] Jacobi studied other Holocaust monuments, taking into account works that came before. After spending time at the USHMM and meeting with US-based Wiesel commissioners, he noted that, '[e]ven though I'd won the national competition, there were some problems and they wanted me to be more literal. We came to a mutual and respectful agreement to disagree'. For instance, commissioners asked Jacobi to include a railway wagon in the design, but he refused, saying that other memorials already did that. Instead, Jacobi created a representation of a railway line inverted into the ground, giving the impression of greater length.

Jacobi shied away from overt representations of death desired by some committee members because he did not want to alienate Romanians from the space. To gain social acceptance, Jacobi said he sought to take the perspective of the Romanian public: 'If I say that Romanians killed, made cadavers, that's what they did, this monument will be rejected'. Instead, he wanted a respectful design for former victims and the present generation of Romanians. Jacobi created what one reviewer described as a 'deliberate alteration of the viewer's sensory data' that 'evokes the abrupt breaking of life and the physical perception of the slipping of time just before death'.[68]

His central memorial building, for instance, with its lined glass roof, suggests a reflective interior space where Jacobi envisioned 'the souls go up'. Six metres tall (around twenty feet), the glass from the ceiling reflecting down for Jacobi 'suggests a deep bottom of six metres. You can imagine a deep hole that can be a grave, it can be symbolistic—an illusionary hole'. As the sun stretches across the sky, shadows on the inside change, creating an illusion of movement, or in Jacobi's words 'the physical impression of time going by—the final moment'. The interplay of time and shadow dominates Jacobi's works. The Star of David sculpture, rising up over eight feet, was constructed to reflect the shadow of itself on the ground on 9 October, Romania's Holocaust Remembrance Day, chosen as the date signifying the beginning of Jewish deportations to Transnistria.

While the committee and Jacobi negotiated the design elements, Nitulescu at the MCC had an ongoing battle to construct the monument. The first was with the General Council of the City of Bucharest, which refused to grant a construction permit for the memorial site.[69] Nitulescu denounced the Bucharest city hall led by mayor Adrian Videanu for the permit failure, claiming that real estate interests planned to profit from the park by converting it into a parking garage.[70]

Second, he was in conflict with environmentalists, led by local NGOs, who argued that the monument's construction would mean the destruction of a public park, an act in violation of the law (in 2005, the government had passed legislation to protect state-controlled green spaces after the sale of public land for private profit reached scandalous proportions). Environmentalists, many of whom were exasperated by the city administration's previous destruction of other Bucharest parks, planned to sue the state to prevent the transformation of the park, accusing the mayor's office of waging a 'genocide against green spaces' by issuing a construction permit that would sacrifice 3,000 square metres of park space.[71]

While public interest in the environmental debate was muted, journalist Ioana Lupea argued that some of the environmentalism masked an unwillingness to come to terms with unpleasant history: '[Many] Romanians don't want a memorial which reminds us of the fact that those who came before us, simple people, gendarmes, soldiers, they humiliated, tortured, deported and killed thousands of innocent people'.[72] Jacobi recalled little overt conflict over his work, but noted that as a *sas* (ethnic German) from Transylvania, he was told, 'Hey German, why don't you do a monument to Germans deported to the former Soviet Union?' After the war, thousands of ethnic Germans from Romania were deported to the USSR as forced labourers in a reparations exchange.[73] Their tragic fate is little remembered by officials, but often mentioned by Romanians as if to obfuscate Holocaust discussions.[74]

The slow construction of the memorial was an embarrassment to Romanian officials travelling abroad. The president, on a visit to Israel, and the foreign minister, on a trip to the United States, faced questions about the memorial's progress. Nearly three years after the initial stone was laid for the memorial, construction began. The recently elected mayor Sorin Oprescu, who had replaced Videanu, told local press that the Romanian Ambassador to America had asked him to find 'a solution for the urgent realization of the monument'.[75] Nitulescu recalled that the stalemate over the construction ended only after Radu Ioanid of the USHMM asked President Băsescu to resolve the delay.[76] Oprescu offered a compromise for environmental concerns: dozens of trees would be transplanted to a nearby park. In the end, the trees were cut and a planned replant was scheduled in a nearby park.[77] Notably, Jacobi offered to pick up the bill for the cost of the trees.[78]

Romani representation in the memorial

Initially, no Roma representatives were on the memorial selection committee and Roma were not incorporated into Jacobi's winning design. Although the Wiesel Commission began its work by including Roma as a victim category, Nitulescu said in an interview that the Romani absence on the committee and in the design was 'an oversight on our part' and Roma were 'worked into the Memorial',[79] with strong support from the USHMM. Paul Shapiro, Director of the Center for Advanced Holocaust Studies at the USHMM, suggested that the low social status of Roma was a hindrance to their public memorialization and urged recognition for their suffering: 'It's important to remember that Roma were also victims of the Antonescu regime. They suffered and died in Transnistria as well'.[80]

Roma appear in three key ways in the memorial structure. There are authorless texts about Roma inscribed around the monument, a list of victims' names inside the memorial building, and a Romani wheel symbol. The Holocaust memorial in Bucharest is, we suggest, a striking paradox. Arguably, in the memorial, Roma are simultaneously *represented*, *unrepresented* and *misrepresented.* Below we describe parts of the memorial and discuss this important paradox.

The experiences of deported Roma are recognized on plaques on the outside of the memorial. The plaques describe the Holocaust experience in Romanian, English and Hebrew. The main text of the memorial, located at the entrance of the memorial structure, reads:

> As the Nazis and their allies and collaborators implemented plans to destroy the Jews of Europe (which would come to be known as the Holocaust or Shoah), the Romanian state unleashed its own systematic persecution of Jews, which was heralded by anti-Semitic legislation of 1940, the pogroms in Dorohoi and Galati in June 1940, as well as those in Bucharest in January 1941 and Iasi in June 1941. Thousands of dead were left behind, and marked the

Figure 1. The memorial structure is the main component of the monument. Behind it is the Ministry of the Interior building that used in 1942, where personnel planned and implemented the persecution of Jews and Roma (copyright Michelle Kelso)

> beginning of the organized destruction of Romanian Jews. In October 1941, the Antonescu regime began to deport Jews from Bessarabia and Bukovina to Transnistria, launching a genocide with the scope of eliminating the country's Jewish population. From 1940–44, the Romanian state was responsible for the deaths of at least 280,000 Romanian and Ukrainian Jews. Also, 25,000 persons of Romani ethnicity were deported to Transnistria, where 11,000 perished . . .

The text, taken in part from the Wiesel report, shaped thereafter by commissioners, and later incorporated into the design by Jacobi, begins with the planned genocide against European Jews by the Nazis and their complicit partners before adding details about the Antonescu regime. The wording is unequivocal, placing responsibility for the deaths of Romanian and Ukrainian Jews squarely on the Romanian authorities.

The Roma segment of the memorial provides a nebulous context that does not help a memorial visitor understand why they were targeted and how so many perished. Of note as well, the Roma genocide, which goes unnamed, has no specific agent: the Romanian state is not clearly identified as a perpetrator of Romani discrimination, deportation and death.

At the back of the Holocaust memorial, a rust-coloured wagon wheel juts out of the ground near the tomb-like structure, and a plaque briefly describes the wheel as a Romani emblem. Rising about two feet off the ground, the wheel is visually unassuming compared to the dramatic Star of David sculpture, which is over eight feet high, and compared to the tallest point of the memorial, a column

Figure 2. The interior of the memorial structure has first names of former Jewish and Romani victims of the Antonescu regime on plaques on the walls (copyright Michelle Kelso)

Figure 3. The Romani wheel symbolizes the Romani people. Thesculpture is located at the back of the monument and is slightly over one foot in height. The column is also pictured on the left (copyright Michelle Kelso)

that rises twenty-three feet into the air and has the Hebrew word for 'remember' carved into it. The wheel, adopted by some Romani activists, is a symbol of Roma migration out of India through Asia into Europe. While the wheel on the monument could symbolize the deportation caravans that carried nomadic Roma to Transnistria, there is no explicit narrative reference on the structure that would lead a viewer to make this link.

However, another plaque does reference how settled Roma were deported to Transnistria. Located on the outside of the moment near the Via Dolorosa, it contains the following inscription: 'During the Holocaust in Romania, freight railcars were used to transport Jews and Roma to their deaths. Many Jews from Bucovina and half of the Roma from the Old Kingdom were deported to Transnistria by train'. The inscription includes an erroneous figure: archival documents of the deportation suggest that about twelve per cent of Roma were deported to Transnistria.[81] The monument's historical narrative omits the fact that, unlike settled Roma, the nomadic Roma were deported not by train but by their own caravans.[82]

Inside the memorial structure, Jewish and Roma first names are featured on plaques hung on three interior stone walls.[83] Jacobi's compromise with the monument committee was not to have a running list of names, as on other memorials, but to display the personalized yet somewhat anonymous first names. Once the decision was made to include Roma on the monument, the former president of the Wiesel Commission asked Viorel Achim, who authored the report's Romani

Figure 4. The Star of David sculpture is over eight feet tall and produces a perfect shadow of the star on the ground on 9 October, Romania's National Holocaust Commemoration Day. The date marks massive deportations of Jews to Transnistria (copyright Michelle Kelso)

chapter, to provide a list of deportee names. In an interview, Achim stated that, 'I went back to the deportation lists and chose the most colourfully ethnic names I found. I didn't want there to be just Ion (John) and Gheorghe (George)'. Jacobi also did an edit of the names for the plaques. Although there is no explanatory text as to whose names are on the walls, the right and left sides display Jewish names (for instance Eva, Frieda, Neoh, Jankel) and the back wall features Romani names, including Busuioc (Basil), Front (Frontline), Diamant (Diamond), and Faron (Pharoh). Presumably, the ethnic nature of some of the names would signify the origin of the victim group for visitors.

We introduced this section of the article with the assertion that Roma are simultaneously *represented*, *unrepresented* and *misrepresented* in Bucharest's Holocaust memorial. Clearly, their victimization is recognized in both the external and internal exhibits and their population losses are made explicit. At the same time, the representation of their experiences is additive in the public narrative: Roma were 'also' victims, but the agents and context of their suffering are not well illuminated. The Romani language is conspicuously absent from the monument, including Romani terms coined for the genocide, *Porrajmos* or *Samudaripen*, suggesting that the structure may speak *for* the Roma but it does not speak *to* them and it does not seek to capture the historical narrative in their cultural voices. In addition, the different experiences of settled and nomadic Roma are obscured by an apparently erroneous figure and the lack of attention to the phenomenon of nomadic Roma, whose deportation experiences have merited little scholarly or political interest.

In the following section, we examine the important question of *why* Roma are marginal actors in Romanian Holocaust history and memorialization and identify three key factors that help to explain this phenomenon.

Romanian Roma: history's marginal actors

Why has the story of Roma victimization in World War II at the hands of Romania's government and sometimes fellow citizens been marginal? What sociological factors account for the relative dearth of Roma experiences and voices in the dominant narrative of Holocaust history and post-communist memorialization? Observers have noted that the wartime decimation and post-war emigration of Jewish communities from Central and Eastern Europe may account for some of the neglect of remembrance of fascist-era atrocities.[84] Young points out that in Poland, for instance, with the decimation of the Jewish community, in the post-war period Poles were 'left alone with their own, uncontested memory of events'.[85] Alas, no such explanation can be applied to the Romanians since the Romani community has grown in the post-war era.[86] Below we look at several reasons for the marginality of Roma and their lack of representation in the texts and memorials of the communist and post-communist periods.

First, Roma memory narratives have remained exclusive and insular, shared within the community but infrequently shared with outsiders and rarely put to paper or published. Roma Holocaust history exists primarily in oral histories in which survivors recount brutal experiences of being forced at gunpoint from their homes, living in misery in the overcrowded barns used to house them, suffering from the ravages of disease and witnessing the death of loved ones. Romani survivors' accounts of their Transnistrian experiences are powerful in their precision about sufferings and tragedies. After 1944, survivors commemorated their dead through the Orthodox tradition of a funerary meal, *pomana*, and by telling their children and grandchildren about *ando Bugo* in Romani, or their deportations to the River Bug. They engaged in counter-memory not as an act of resistance, but as an act of being.

While Jewish survivors and anti-communist dissidents in Romania had a testimony boom after 1989,[87] Roma have rarely entered public space with their stories. With little education and few opportunities to study existing history texts or even documentaries (many of which are not in Romanian and are subtitled, excluding illiterate survivors from the potential audience), Roma would also have had little opportunity to fully grasp the dominant narratives of Holocaust history—or their exclusion from them. Nonetheless, Roma interviewees present thoughtful understandings of their sufferings and ascribe culpability to two men: 'Hitler and Antonescu'. Survivor Silvia Stanescu asks, for example: 'Hitler, what did he have against Gypsies and Jews?'[88]

Romani survivors, for the most part, have not tended to advocate for educational initiatives to explain their suffering. While this may seem counter to advancing the status of the Romani minority, survivors like Ion Tanase point out that 'everyone knows what happened to us'.[89] Tanase believed this because of the rampant anti-Romani rhetoric used by many Romanians. From football team fans to neighbours, Roma interviewees suggest that it is not uncommon to hear Romanians lament Antonescu's failure to rid the country of all its Gypsies: *Too bad Antonescu didn't finish what he started.*[90] Tanase also believed that little would change in post-communist Romania, where in the early 1990s some forty villages burned Roma out of their homes in acts of ethnic violence.[91]

Second, the internment and killing of Roma by Romanians has been particularly challenging to weave into Romanian historical narratives, as well as the contemporary social order. It is not only a counter-narrative that departs from the more canonic European story of Jews as the victims of Holocaust atrocities, but it also inverts commonly held assumptions among the majority of ethnic Romanians that members of the Roma minority are victimizing them with their ostensibly deviant behaviours.[92] Roma appear in mainstream historical and contemporary narratives in a particular social role: according to a World Bank report issued in 2005, most Romanians believe that Roma are social deviants (criminals).[93] The Roma are thus 'unruly actors' in the post-Wiesel report narrative of the national past. Eglitis and Zelce define unruly actors as 'historical actors who are challenges to dominant memory narratives because they fail to conform to socially ascribed roles and norms', suggesting that 'the marginality of some groups in dominant narratives of history can be understood in terms of their disruption of the historical "scene", which is configured to reflect and reproduce a social order that benefits politically and socially powerful groups or institutions in society'.[94] In this instance, Roma, defined in dominant narratives as deviants—indeed, as victimizers of Romanians—appear unexpectedly as innocent victims of a genocidal regime, disrupting the mainstream distribution of social roles and a longstanding historical narrative in which Romanian victimization was at the centre and Roma victimization was unrecognized.

Third, for communities characterized by economic deprivation and struggle, public commemoration may be an economic luxury that they forgo to focus on immediate needs. Arguably, pursuit of the public good of historical commemoration is influenced by class position and those with greater cultural, social and economic capital are relatively more likely to both seek and receive recognition. Following Bourdieu's concept of symbolic violence—that is, the process by which social groups exclude themselves from roles and practices from which they would be structurally excluded—we might hypothesize that the Roma community does not actively endeavour to seek that from which they have historically been excluded, including recognition of their plight in cultural productions such as museums, monuments, books and media. Their economic marginality has pointed them towards a pursuit of restitution rather than recognition. During Kelso's fieldwork, she found that many lived in distressed rural areas, supported by their children. A few survived on miniscule state pensions; some worked well into old age as day labourers or in traditional trades. Roma have the lowest rates of academic attainment, the highest rates of infant mortality, the worst housing situations and the most dramatic rates of unemployment of any ethnic group in Europe.[95] In the post-communist period, Roma have been most interested in receiving compensation from the Romanian state for their deportation and incarceration, as well as for the expropriation of their property and goods. Their desires are likely also driven by Romania's efforts to return property confiscated by the state under communism to former owners and their heirs, a continuing programme that is one of the most comprehensive in former Eastern bloc countries.

Conclusion

Roma have long been on the margins of Romanian society and history. Their marginality can be understood as the outcome of a confluence of long-existing and contemporary factors. Low levels of formal education and a deficit of economic resources at the individual and community levels have combined with marginal social status to deprive Roma of a public voice. No less notably, Roma appear in dominant public narratives as victimizers—thieves and bandits—rather than victims;[96] the inversion of this order casts them in the role of unruly actors, playing a role that challenges powerful normative assumptions about Roma. Recently, Roma activists and non-Roma advocates have challenged the forces of marginalization. The Holocaust memorial in Bucharest is, in a sense, a monument to both change and stasis in Roma representation, offering a new public recognition of victimization while affirming the community's still-subordinate social position.

The memorial offers a foundation for the development of a more complex, nuanced public narrative of the past. Sociologist Jean Baudrillard writes that '[f]orgetting the extermination is part of the extermination itself'.[97] Indeed, the post-war and early post-communist periods in Romania were, arguably, triumphs of forgetting over remembering in the construction of a national narrative. The last decade has, by contrast, broken open the field of historical memory, providing an opening for new actors to join the effort to construct a public narrative of the past. While the Roma remain marginal in many respects, they are no longer invisible. Indeed remembering the past and memorializing its victims in order to avoid repeating the crimes of history may be too important in Romania—and across the continent—to leave the writing of history only to the powerful.

Endnotes

1 This charge is also inscribed on the monument.
2 Speech by President Traian Băsescu, Unveiling of the Holocaust memorial (Bucharest, Romania), 8 October 2009, available at: http://www.presidency.ro/ (retrieved 8 August 2013).
3 Michel-Rolph Trouillot, *Silencing the past: power and the production of history* (Boston: Beacon Press, 1997).
4 Nina Tumarkin, *The living and the dead: the rise and fall of the cult of World War II in Russia* (New York: Basic Books, 1994).
5 Jeffrey Olick (ed.), 'Introduction', in *States of memory: continuities, conflicts, and transformations in national retrospection* (Durham: Duke University Press, 2003), p. 8; see also Daina Eglitis, *Imagining the nation: history, modernity and revolution in Latvia* (University Park: Pennsylvania State University Press, 2002).

6 James Mark, *The unfinished revolution: making sense of the communist past in Central-Eastern Europe* (New Haven: Yale University Press, 2010), pp. 66–67.
7 As James Mark points out, as late as 2006 a Presidential Commission was writing a report to decisively condemn the communist experience and to frame the 1989 revolution as 'anti-communist' rather than specifically 'anti-Ceauşescu'. He writes: 'The establishment of the Presidential Commission rested on the assumption that Romania needed to reject its communist past fully in order to assure its liberal democratic future, and that the creation of a new state-sponsored official memory to which the political elite and wider population could adhere was the best way to secure it' (*The unfinished revolution*, p. 33). See also pp. 32–46.
8 Maurice Halbwachs, *On collective memory*, ed. and trans. Lewis A. Coser (Chicago: University of Chicago Press, 1992).
9 Richard Ned Lebow, 'The memory of politics in postwar Europe', in Richard Ned Lebow, Wulf Kansteiner and Claudio Fogu (eds.), *The politics of memory in postwar Europe* (Durham: Duke University Press, 2006), pp.1–39.
10 Pierre Bourdieu, *The field of cultural production* (New York: Columbia University Press, 1993). See also Bourdieu, *The rules of art: genesis and structure of the literary field* (Palo Alto: Stanford University Press, 1996).
11 Eric Langenbacher, 'Twenty-first century memory regimes in Germany and Poland', *German Politics and Society*, Vol. 26, No. 4, 2008, p. 53.
12 See Radu Ioanid, Michelle Kelso and Luminita Cioaba (eds.), *Tragedia romilor deportati in Transnistria, 1942–1945: marturii si documente* (Iaşi: Polirom, 2009).
13 See Jean Ancel, 'The German-Romanian relationship and the final solution', *Holocaust and Genocide Studies*, Vol. 19, No. 2, 2005, pp. 252–275; Dennis Deletant, 'Ghetto experience in Golta, Transnistria, 1942–1944', *Holocaust and Genocide Studies*, Vol. 18, No. 1, 2004, pp. 1–26; Vladimir Solonari, 'An important new document on the Romanian policy of ethnic cleansing during World War II', *Holocaust and Genocide Studies*, Vol. 21, No. 2, 2007, pp. 268–297; Rebecca L. Golbert, 'Holocaust sites in Ukraine: Pechora and the politics of memorialization', *Holocaust and Genocide Studies*, Vol. 18, 2004, pp. 205–233.Viorel Achim, *The Roma in Romanian history* (Budapest: Central European University Press, 2004).
14 Achim, *The Roma in Romanian history*; Solonari, 'An important new document', pp. 268–297.
15 Tuvia Friling, Radu Ioanid and Mihail E. Ionescu, *Final report of the international commission on the Holocaust Romania* (Iaşi: Polirom Publishing, 2005), p. 120.
16 Radu Ioanid, *Holocaustul in Romania. Distrugerea evreilor si romilor sub regimul Antonescu 1940–1944* (Bucharest: Hasefer, 2006), p. 177.
17 File Preşedinţia Consiliului de Mini̧ştri, 292/1941, p. 3: Romanian National Archives.
18 Viorel Achim, *Ţiganii în istoria României* (Bucharest: Editura Enciclopedică, 1998).
19 File Preşedinţia Consiliului de Mini̧ştri, 42/1942, p. 2: Romanian National Archives.
20 Prior to the acquisition of Transnistria, Antonescu considered internal work camps for Roma, and also deporting them internally to an under-populated region. See Michael Benjamin Thorne, 'Assimilation, invisibility, and the eugenic turn in the "Gypsy question" in Romanian society, 1938–1942', *Romani Studies*, Vol. 21, No. 2, 2011, pp. 177–205.
21 Achim, *Ţiganii în istoria României*; Michelle Kelso, 'Gypsy deportations from Romania to Transnistria 1942–1944', in Donald Kenrick (ed.), *The Gypsies during the second world war: in the shadow of the swastika*, 2 Vols. (Hatfield: University of Hertfordshire Press, 1999), 2: pp. 95–130.
22 Kelso, 'Gypsy deportations', p. 109.
23 Radu Ioanid, *Evreii sub regimul Antonescu* (Bucharest: Editura Hasefer, 1997), pp. 316–321.
24 File Inspectorat General al Jandarmerie, 126/1942, p. 26: Romanian National Archives.
25 File Inspectorat General al Jandarmerie, 126/1942, p. 205: Romanian National Archives.
26 File Inspectorat General al Jandarmerie 130/1942, pp. 127–131: Romanian National Archives.
27 Achim, *The Roma in Romanian history*, p. 141.
28 Kelso 'Gypsy deportations', p. 112.
29 Kelso 'Gypsy deportations', p. 121.
30 Under communism nomadism became illegal.
31 Interview with Lucia Mihai. Interviewer: Survivors of the Shoah Visual History Foundation. Available at: http://vhf.ushmm.org/ (retrieved 10 February 2010). Accessible at institutions that subscribe to the VHF database.
32 *Final Report* states that 11,000 Roma died. The figure was reached using documents from the Transnistria administration before liberation. Oral testimony, however, suggests that many died on the road back to Romania. As such, it is likely that the *Final Report* underestimates the number of deaths.
33 Randolph L. Braham, 'The exculpatory history of Romanian nationalists: the exploitation of the Holocaust for political ends', in Randolph Braham (ed.), *The destruction of Romanian and Ukrainian Jews during the*

Antonescu era (New York: Columbia University Press, 1997), pp.49–50.; Adrian Cioflancă, 'A "grammar of exculpation" in communist historiography: distortion of the history of the Holocaust under Ceauşescu', *Romanian Journal of Political Sciences*, Vol. 2, 2004, pp. 29–46.
34 Mark, *The unfinished revolution*, p. 94.
35 Alexandru Florian, 'The perception of the Holocaust in historiography and in the Romanian media', in Valentina Glajar and Jeanine Teodorescu (eds.), *Local history, transnational memory in the Romanian Holocaust* (New York: Palgrave Macmillan, 2011), pp. 19–45.
36 Katherine Verdery, *National ideology* under socialism : identity and cultural politics in Ceauşescu's Romania (Berkeley: University of California Press, 1991), p. 8.
37 Verdery, *National ideology*, p. 220.
38 Friling, Ioanid and Ionescu, *Final report*, pp. 15–16.
39 Friling, Ioanid and Ionescu, *Final report*, pp. 17–18.
40 Florian, 'The perception of the Holocaust', pp. 27–29.
41 Mark, *The unfinished revolution*, p. 94.
42 Ordonanţa de Urgenţă 31.2002, Monitorul Oficial de Romaniei, available at: http://www.monitoruloficial.ro/ (retrieved 7 April 2008).
43 'Mari Romani', available at: www.mariromani.ro (retrieved 6 July 2007).
44 'Fenomenul discriminarii in România. Sondaj de opinie', Elie Wiesel National Institute for the Study of the Holocaust in Romania, November 2010, pp. 10–11.
45 Dominica Radulescu, 'Elie Wiesel's night: the death of hope and Romania's problematic moral stand in relation to the Holocaust', in Glajar and Teodorescu, *Local history*, pp. 195–196. The phrase 'haven for Jews' is from Radu Ioanid, *The Holocaust in Romania* (Chicago: Ivan R. Dee, 2000), p. xi.
46 Mihai Chioveanu, 'A deadlock of memory: the myth and cult of Ion Antonescu in post-communist Romania', *Studia Hebraica*, Vol. 3, 2003, pp. 102–137.
47 Lawrence Weinbaum, 'The banality of history and memory: Romanian society and the Holocaust', 2006, available at: http://www.jewishvirtuallibrary.org/jsource/Holocaust/Romania_Holo.html (retrieved 15 July 2013).
48 Aro Velmet, 'Occupied identities: national narratives in Baltic museums of occupations', *Journal of Baltic Studies*, Vol. 42, No. 2, 2011, p. 197.
49 See Edward Linenthal, *Preserving memory: the struggle to create America's Holocaust museum*, 2nd edn. (New York: Columbia University Press, 2001).
50 Friling, Ioanid and Ionescu, *Final report*.
51 Many of the reports' authors had previously published books or articles in Romania about the topics they wrote on for the report.
52 Friling, Ioanid and Ionescu, *Final report*, p. 389.
53 James E. Young, *The texture of memory: Holocaust memorials and meaning* (New Haven: Yale University Press, 1993).
54 As Bourdieu and Wacquant describe it, 'a field is simultaneously a space of conflict and competition ... in which participants vie to establish monopoly over the species of capital effective in it ... and the power to decree their hierarchy and "conversion rates" between all forms of authority in the field of power', in Pierre Bourdieu and Lois Wacquant, *An invitation to reflexive sociology* (Chicago: University of Chicago Press, 1992), p. 17.
55 Razvan Paraianu, 'The history textbooks controversy in Romania. Five years on', Eurozone, 2005, available at: http://www.eurozine.com/articles/2005-11-11-paraianu-en.html (retrieved 9 August 2010); see Michael Shafir, 'Denying the Holocaust where it happened: post-communist denial in East Central Europe and the Shoah', in Ronit Lentin (ed.), *Re-presenting the Shoah for the 21st century* (New York and Oxford: Berghahn Books, 2002), pp. 195–226.
56 Michelle Kelso, '"And Roma were victims, too": the Romani genocide and Holocaust education in Romania', *Intercultural Education*, Vol. 24, Nos. 1–2, 2013, pp. 61–78.
57 Ana Bărbulescu, Laura Degeratu and Cosmina Gusu, 'The Holocaust as reflected in communist and post-communist Romanian textbooks', *Intercultural Education*, Vol. 24, Nos. 1–2, 2013, pp. 41–60.
58 Mark, *The unfinished revolution*, p. 96. Romania is a relative latecomer to this trend, however. Early adopters of the Western model of Holocaust remembrance were the Baltic countries, who established history commissions in the 1990s, although the embrace of the model is incomplete.
59 'Romania facing its past', USHMM, available at: http://www.ushmm.org/research/scholarly-presentations/symposia/holocaust-in-romania/romania-facing-its-past (retrieved 11 August 2013).
60 'ADL calls Romanian ministry's remarks on Holocaust "outrageous," urges government to come to terms with history', Press Release, Anti-Defamation League, available at: http://archive.adl.org/PresRele/HolNa_52/4270_52.htm (retrieved 8 August 2013).

61 See Council of Europe's website for more details: http://www.coe.int/t/dg3/romatravellers/default_en.asp (retrieved 11 August 2013).
62 Shafir, 'Denying the Holocaust'.
63 Shafir, 'Denying the Holocaust', p. 202.
64 Interview with Florin Manole. Interviewer: Michelle Kelso. Bucharest, Romania, June 2013.
65 Interview with Marian Mandache. Interviewer: Michelle Kelso. Bucharest, Romania, June 2013.
66 Paraianu, 'The history textbooks'.
67 Interview with Peter Jacobi. Interviewer: Michelle Kelso. Bucharest, Romania, June 2013.
68 Magda Predescu, 'A new concept of urban sculpture', available at: http://www.peterhjacobi.de/peter_jacobi.htm (retrieved 24 June 2013).
69 'Memorialul Holocaustului, intre ecologie si imaginea Romaniei', Evenimentul Zilei, 18 May 2009, available at: http://www.evz.ro/detalii/stiri/memorialul-holocaustului-intre-ecologie-si-imaginea-romaniei-851406.html (retrieved 20 May 2013); 'Constructia Monumentului Holocaustului, blocata de consiliul general Bucuresti', Hotnews, 15 January 2008, available at: http://www.hotnews.ro/stiri-cultura-2197108-constructia-monumentului-holocaustului-blocata-consiliul-general-bucuresti.htm (retrieved 10 June 2013).
70 'Memorialul Holocaustului', Evenimentul Zilei; 'Constructia Monumentului Holocaustului', Hotnews.
71 'Memorialul Holocaustului, Evenimentul Zilei; 'Constructia Monumentului Holocaustului', Hotnews.
72 Ioana Lupea, 'Nu vedem Holocaustul din cauza copacilor', Realitatea.net, 12 May 2009, available at: http://www.realitatea.net/ioana-lupea–nu-vedem-holocaustul-din-cauza-copacilor_516086.html (retrieved 15 March 2013).
73 See Jill Massino, 'Gender as survival: women's experiences of deportation from Romania to the Soviet Union, 1945–1950', *Nationalities Papers*, Vol. 36, No. 1, 2008, pp. 55–83.
74 Kelso found repeatedly in her fieldwork that academics, teachers and average Romanians tried to persuade her that the deportations of ethnic Germans were 'a better and real topic' of study, implying that examining Romani deportations to Transnistria was not a valid subject of academic pursuit.
75 'Bucuresti: primaria capitalei va muta 30 de copaci pentru monumentul holocaustului', Adevarul, 29 April 2009, available at: adevarul.ro/news/societate/bucuresti-primaria-capitalei-muta-30-copaci-monumentul-holocaustului-1_50acd75b7c42d5a6638a827a/index.html (retrieved 15 June 2013).
76 Interview with Virgil Nitulescu. Interviewer: Michelle Kelso. Bucharest, Romania, June 2013.
77 'Monumentul Holocaustului: In loc sa fie transplantati, cei 32 de arbori au fost taiati cu drujba', Hotnews, 5 June 2009, available at: http://www.hotnews.ro/stiri-esential-5792006-monumentul-holocaustului-loc-fie-transplantati-cei-32-arbori-fost-taiati-drujba.htm (retrieved 14 May 2013).
78 Nitulescu interview.
79 Nitulescu interview.
80 Interview with Paul Shapiro. Interviewer: Michelle Kelso. Washington, DC, November 2009.
81 Friling, Ioanid and Ionescu, *Final report*; Kelso, 'Gypsy deportations'.
82 Kelso, 'Gypsy deportations', pp. 101–106.
83 Interview with Viorel Achim. Interviewer: Michelle Kelso. Bucharest, Romania, June 2013.
84 Mark, *The unfinished revolution*, p. 94.
85 Young, *The texture of memory*, p. 116.
86 The October 2011 Romanian census showed that the Romani population had increased since the last census.
87 Stefan Ionescu, 'The boom of testimonies after communism: the voices of the Jewish Holocaust survivors in Romania (1989–2005)', *Studia Hebraica*, Vol. 5, 2005, pp. 357–380.
88 Michelle Kelso, 'Introducere', in Radu Ioanid, Michelle Kelso and Luminiţa Cioabă (eds.), *Tragedia romilor deportati in Transnistria, 1942–1945: marturii si documente* (Iaşi: Polirom, 2009), p. 25.
89 Interview with Ion Tanase. Interviewer: Michelle Kelso. Mereni de Jos, Romania, 15 October 1999.
90 Michelle Kelso, 'Hidden history: perceptions of the Romani Holocaust viewed through contemporary race relations', *Anthropology of East Europe Review*, Vol. 25, No. 2, 2007, pp. 44–61.
91 David Crowe, 'The Gypsies in Romania since 1990', Nationalities Papers, Vol. 27, No. 1, 1999, pp. 57–67.
92 Kelso, 'Introducere', pp. 30–31.
93 'Final report: qualitative survey (focus groups) attitudes towards the Roma in Romania', World Bank, 2005, available at: http://web.worldbank.org/WBSITE/EXTERNAL/COUNTRIES/ECAEXT/EXTROMA/0,,contentMDK:20749979~pagePK:64168445~piPK:64168309~theSitePK:615987,00.html (retrieved 7 July 2010).
94 Daina S. Eglitis and Vita Zelce, 'Unruly actors: Latvian women of the red army in post-war historical memory', *Nationalities Papers*, Vol. 41, No. 6, 2013, pp. 987–1007.
95 Andrey Ivanov and Antonia Zheliazkova, *Roma in central and eastern Europe:* avoiding the dependency trap (Bratislava: United Nations Development Programme, Regional Bureau for Europe and the Commonwealth of Independent States, 2002); 'Faces of poverty, faces of hope', United Nations Development Programme,

Bratislava, 2005, available at: http://europeandcis.undp.org/public/show/67D47F90-F203-1EE9-BB4A88AD1FF2FF8D (retrieved 10 January 2008).

96 World Bank, 'Final report', available at: http://hdr.undp.org/sites/default/files/avoiding_the_dependency_trap_en.pdf.

97 Jean Baudrillard, *Simulacra and simulation* (Ann Arbor: University of Michigan Press, 1995), p. 49.

Revisiting the El Mozote massacre: memory and politics in postwar El Salvador

RAFAEL ALARCÓN MEDINA and LEIGH BINFORD

In December 1981, the Salvadoran Atlacatl Battalion massacred more than a thousand men, women and children in and around the rural hamlet of El Mozote in Morazán Department during a scorched earth operation at the beginning of the Salvadoran civil war. The main massacre site has been the setting for commemorations, memorials and murals and attracts large numbers of national and international tourists. This article explores the way in which the history of El Mozote and its articulation with El Salvador's civil war history has been framed by different groups. We discuss the complexities of memory, politics and the place of the El Mozote massacre in postwar El Salvador in the context of Morazán's insurgent past and suggest, following Walter Benjamin, that the contested meaning of the massacre rises from the contradictory praxis of actors struggling to develop hegemony over the ways in which this event is/will be remembered and why.

Pa'llorar por los que han muerto somos todos muy valientes
Pa'llorar por los que han muerto siempre hay muchísima gente
Pero el morir por los pueblos es una cosa de locos
Para morir por los pueblos hay muy pocos hay muy pocos
Y buscamos los culpables cuando matan un valiente
Y buscamos los culpables cuando muere un inocente
No fueron los asesinos fuimos nosotros
Que los dejamos morir por ser tan pocos[1]

—Tabaré Etcheverry

Introduction

In 1992, peace accords ended a twelve-year civil war in El Salvador that resulted in at least 75,000 deaths and 7,000 disappearances. Over two decades later, Salvadorans still struggle with the war's meaning and its place in the country's history. The 1981 massacre at El Mozote has become a central part of that process. On 16 January 2012, Mauricio Funes, the first president from the Frente Farabundo Martí de Liberación Nacional Party (Farabundo Martí National Liberation Front, FMLN), travelled to El Mozote to officially acknowledge the responsibility of the Salvadoran state in the massacre and to ask forgiveness from the survivors and the victims' families.[2] Funes' state apology was preceded by almost three decades of official denial of the massacre by conservative administrations, a claim that was always contested by many Morazanians, Salvadorans elsewhere and supporters abroad. In the end, people from Morazán and their national and international allies took the case to the Inter-American Court of Human Rights for trial. On 25 October 2012, the Court ruled in the victims' favour, ordering the Salvadoran state to investigate the massacre and enact a variety of symbolic and economic reparations.[3] The analysis of the complexities of the trial and the sentence fall beyond the scope of this article. Here we focus on the complex web of social relations that revolve around and shape the meaning and political importance of the El Mozote massacre and its memorial site for postwar El Salvador and, in particular, for the inhabitants of northern Morazán.

Mark Danner's *The massacre at El Mozote* provides the most widely known English-language account of the massacre. In a lengthy article in the January 1993 issue of *The New Yorker* magazine, which was quickly transformed into a book, Danner wrote that, between 11 and 13 December 1981, the Atlacatl Battalion, under the command of Lieutenant Colonel Domingo Monterrosa, slaughtered approximately one thousand people (men, women and children) in El Mozote and six other hamlets located near the command post of the Ejercito Revolucionario de Pueblo (People's Revolutionary Army, ERP) faction of the FMLN.[4] A few days earlier, according to Danner, Marcos Díaz, a local leader, had relayed a message from the army that if all the people in the surrounding countryside gathered in the centre of El Mozote, known as *El Llano* (The Plain), their lives would be spared when the coming military operation swept the area for FMLN guerrillas. Díaz also reportedly stated that his contact in the military had told him that people who remained in their homes in outlying areas would be killed. Díaz himself died in the massacre, a victim of the false information that he transmitted. *The massacre at El Mozote* proved of great importance in disseminating knowledge of the event a dozen years after it took place and in critically detailing the role of United States officials in covering it up. But although he had little—almost nothing in fact—to say about El Mozote's pre-war history, Danner did portray the residents as politically neutral evangelical Protestants, casting a pale of innocence on the victims, who, as a purported consequence of their religious beliefs, would not have joined revolutionaries.[5] The belief that the dead were mostly evangelicals is accepted, even today, by the FMLN, probably because it enhances the image of brutality of the army, which seemed incapable (or uninterested) in discriminating between supporters and opposition.

Tutela Legal, the Catholic Archbishop's legal aid organization, took up the matter in 1990, when several survivors filed a complaint in the departmental capital of San Francisco Gotera. It has produced detailed reports of the events based on eyewitness testimony but has contributed little to our knowledge of the victims' pre-war experiences or their political sympathies.[6] Surveying the extant literature led Binford to suggest that the human rights discourse fuelling international interest in El Mozote (and similar cases) erases El Mozote's complex history.[7] He argued that before the war, El Mozote was a growing rural hub with steady economic development, a point that is ignored in most accounts of the massacre even among people in northern Morazán.[8] Today, El Mozote is mostly known for its history of blood, death and darkness, an image that has become a strategic ideological construction that may aid people in the affected hamlets in their struggle for material reparations, tourism and economic development.

The construction of El Mozote as a unified, peaceful and innocent community at the time of the massacre also played an important role in the discourse presented by lawyers and expert witnesses acting on behalf of the victims in the Inter-American Court tribunal in Guayaquil, Ecuador in April 2012. For instance, expert witness psychologist Sol Yáñez spoke of the *Sujeto Colectivo* (collective subject) that was destroyed in the massacre. The idea of a collective subject references pre-war El Mozote as an 'innocent' and unified community, unaffiliated with the rebels and absent internal class divisions that might generate sympathy for the FMLN and attract recruits to the FMLN cause. In Morazán and elsewhere, that image has been enhanced by the representation of pre-war El Mozote as predominantly populated by Evangelicals who were markedly unsympathetic to FMLN efforts to overthrow a military-led government.[9] However, the balance of evidence indicates that before the war the residents of El Mozote, and perhaps other affected hamlets, were *both* Catholic *and* politically conservative, in part because the resident catechist, José Carmen Romero, remained under the thumb of reactionary priest Fa. Andrés Argueta, charged with religious affairs in Jocoaitique parish to which the affected hamlets were ecclesiastically affiliated. Finally, those who repopulated the El Mozote area eschew detailed discussion of the community's past, particularly of embryonic class divisions between petty bourgeoisie merchants, middle peasants and the land poor and landless. Lists containing occupational information on the dead indicate that fifty per cent had been *jornaleros* (day labourers) compared to sixteen per cent *campesinos* (landed peasants). Day labourers often rented land from others, but they also sold their labour power regionally and migrated to agro-export zones during cotton, coffee and sugar harvests. Another sixteen per cent worked as maguey spinners, paid by the task for spinning maguey fibre into twine. In short, El Mozote and the surrounding area was experiencing an incipient process of rural social differentiation, which had accelerated in the years before the war with the introduction of machines for extracting maguey fibre and crushing sugar cane.[10] The tensions that this process generated, most sharply expressed when people were under the influence of alcohol, have been forgotten by most people. The immensity of wartime death and destruction combined with a decade-long displacement to skew memory of life in pre-war El Mozote towards a nostalgic vision of an idealized past.

Existing between the real and the mythical, then, the history of El Mozote is being reframed and, with it, so is its articulation with El Salvador's civil war history. In order to understand the complexities of memory, politics and the place of the El Mozote massacre in postwar El Salvador, we need to examine Morazán's insurgent past. The contested meaning of the massacre arises from the contradictory praxis of actors struggling to develop hegemony over the ways in which this event is/will be remembered and why. The state, survivors, victims' relatives and people in El Mozote are at centre stage in this story. However, as we argue below, in the background, behind the official actors, there are former combatants, FMLN supporters and their organizations, for whom the El Mozote massacre stands as a contradictory image of the past around which they elaborate and develop their own particular labours of memory about their place in the recent insurgent history of El Salvador.[11] In this article, we discuss two of these organizations (CEBES and PRODETUR) and their construction of massacre memorialization in Morazán and El Salvador. We begin with a historical overview of these actors and their relations with the massacre's history and memory of it. Next, we discuss the memorial site, El Mozote and the various ways that people there confront its dark history. Finally, we draw on the work of Walter Benjamin in proposing an active interpretation of memory as a condensation of social struggles and point to the relevance of this contestation to the postwar present and future of El Mozote, northern Morazán and El Salvador.[12]

CEBES

The antecedents of CEBES extend back to the late 1960s, when Father José Inocencio Alas founded the first Ecclesiastic Base Communities of El Salvador in the department of Suchitoto.[13] But the immediate roots of what became CEBES were developed before the war by priests (mostly Belgian) and nuns (Salvadoran) labouring in the working class community of Zacamil in San Salvador. The priests scattered—some to exile in Nicaragua, others to Costa Rica or the United States—as repression against the church intensified, while the nuns remained in the capital. CEBES developed as a means of sustaining contact among these groups and keeping alive the Base Community movement. The nuns served as liaisons, crossing national borders and the frontiers between government and guerrilla zones in order to share information, distribute resources and coordinate work. Fa. Rogelio Ponceele was among these Zacamil veterans. Following the murder of one priest and death threats against others, in 1980 he abandoned his post in the capital.[14] But rather than going into exile, Ponceele travelled to Morazán under ERP escort and spent the entirety of the war offering mass, marrying couples, baptizing children and burying civilians and combatants alike under the thunder and fire of air assaults and ground invasions, supported by the United States government's counter-insurgency policies in Latin America.[15] CEBES remained active in northern Morazán in the postwar period, although not with the same force in all municipalities. Through catechism classes, in Ponceele's sermons and myriad other activities, CEBES continues to spread Christian teachings with a strong political engagement and coordinates much work with local FMLN political structures, albeit maintaining distance and autonomy. However, this ongoing relationship means that many people who disagree with the FMLN's political ideology or who abandoned the zone during the war identify CEBES with northern Morazán's conflict-ridden past, including Seventh Day Adventists, Evangelicals, Jehovah's Witnesses and conservative Catholic followers of Fa. Argueta and more recently Fa. Juan José del Cid, who replaced Argueta in 2006 following the elder prelate's death.

This issue is accentuated by the ERP-FMLN's wartime suppression of non-Catholic religious beliefs and practices. As refugees and displaced persons returned to Morazán after the war, the political and religious fields grew more heterogeneous and complex. CEBES' organizational strength diminished significantly and is now mostly limited to former FMLN combatants, supporters and their families in Perquín, San Fernando, Torola, Villa El Rosario and large portions of the repopulated Segundo Montes community. After the war, Father Rogelio and his team continued their political organizational efforts, but the turn to the right in the Salvadoran Catholic Church meant that Ponceele's (and, by extension, CEBES') range of influence has diminished. The return of the ultra-conservative Father Andrés Argueta to Jocoaitique in the early 1990s eroded Ponceele's authority in places like El Mozote. Regardless, CEBES played a central role in sponsoring annual commemorations of the massacre, beginning in 1991, and worked with Tutela Legal to bring the El Mozote massacre case before the Inter-American Court of Human Rights in 2012. The commemorative activities and the constructions that CEBES has sponsored or supported in the form of monuments, murals, gardens and other forms of material culture sustain the human rights value and enhance the touristic value of the site.

PRODETUR

Apart from its wartime alliance with the progressive church, the ERP-FMLN encouraged the creation of producers' cooperatives in its northern Morazanian rearguard. Such organizations played important roles in the war effort, providing rebel troops with food, information about government troop movements, and logistical services (bearing wounded combatants to clandestine hospitals and smuggling batteries, boots and other goods into the zone).[16] They represented one side of the contested hegemony of the FMLN in opposition to the Salvadoran state, in a few cases establishing de facto parallel forms of government. In Morazán, organizations like the Community Development Council of Morazán and San Miguel (Patronato para el Desarrollo de las Comunidades de Morazán y San Miguel, PADECOMSM) and, towards the end of the war, the productive cooperatives in Segundo Montes City (Ciudad Segundo Montes, CSM), formed part of this organizational effort.[17] However, by 2012, most collective organizations had collapsed, victims of internal contradictions exacerbated by two decades of neoliberal political economy. One of the few initiatives that muddled along was the Tourism Promoter (Promotora de Turismo, PRODETUR), conceived during the last years of the war but concretized only after it ended.

PRODETUR has a politically varied membership, but the leadership consists overwhelmingly of former ERP combatants who identify with the FMLN. This organization depends on international sponsors for its funding, and its main goals are to protect the environment and promote northern Morazán as a tourist destination. Reputed to have been one of the hottest and most dangerous regions during the civil war, Morazán is now being marketed nationally and internationally as the *Ruta de Paz* (Peace Route). With much of the country immersed in quotidian violence related to the *maras* (Salvadoran gangs) and other kinds of everyday violence that escalated following the end of armed conflict, contemporary northern Morazán is one of the safest places to visit.[18] Also, twelve years of death, destruction and displacement followed by postwar out-migration reduced northern Morazán's population at least forty per cent below its pre-war level, contributing to the spread of anthropogenic forests that appeal to ecotourists.[19] Of concern in this article, however, is the central role of Morazán's recent insurgent history in the contemporary touristic agenda and in particular the role El Mozote plays in that agenda.

Visitors travelling from San Francisco Gotera to Perquín on the *Calle Negra*, the Black Street, encounter a series of signs announcing the Peace Route, one of five tourism routes through which El Salvador's Ministry of Tourism markets the nation's beaches, archaeological sites and history. The transformation of revolutionary history into a commoditized discourse is expressed in different ways. In the case of PRODETUR, it is manifest in the way former combatants have transitioned into tour guides who take visitors on a journey back in time as they walk along forest paths and encounter civil war battle settings, destroyed trenches and sentry posts. At the top of *Cerro Pericón* (Pericon Hill), a militarily strategic position hotly contested during the war, guides describe the army's wartime movements and guerrilla efforts to deter the soldiers. Stories of FMLN heroism abound. The guides deploy an alienated form of experience of the past in which revolutionary struggle is transformed into an entertaining adventure tale absent the pain, pathos and suffering of combatants or civilians. The tour ends with the guides condemning armed struggle in favour of dialogue and the defence of human rights. The density and complexity of the Salvadoran revolution becomes reduced to a superficial story.

Between CEBES' role in taking the case to the Inter-American Court and PRODETUR's efforts to give the El Mozote massacre a key place in its touristic agenda, there lies the El Mozote massacre memorial site itself and the particular ways in which people there confront their past.

El Mozote nunca más: a mythical community under the discourse of human rights

It is closing in on midday in El Mozote. A small group of women sit under the shade of a tree in front of a tourist kiosk next to the town plaza. They are knitting placemats or making bracelets, earrings and necklaces from seeds and bits of coconut shell. The plaza is the community's central neuronal space, reached by traversing an access road that connects El Mozote to the Arambala-Joateca route. Even now, thirty years later, this epicentre of the massacre, albeit repopulated, feels abandoned. Only a few people gather on the streets. In front of the park, a recently constructed cinder block chalet sells sodas, chips and a few handicraft items. On the opposite side of the plaza from the store the eye takes in an elaborate monument in the form of a wooden wall with small plaques inscribed with the names of people slaughtered by the Atlacatl Battalion in December 1981. A few metres south of the monument and up a small rise lies the Church of the Three Kings and the Garden of the Innocents, which also form part of the memorial site.

During our visits to El Mozote we have become accustomed to seeing buses, vans and automobiles disgorging students, church delegations, foreign tourists and families. On one such visit (2 July 2012), a group of American high school students arrive to learn about the massacre. Once their bus has been parked, the local women sitting near the kiosk stand and approach the group. They are the official guides to the site. In this case, however, the students have brought their own guide—also an American—who explains the events that took place here at some distance from the main monument. The guides sit back down and wait while the foreign students take a short tour around other historical places in El Mozote: the house of Israel Márquez, where women were killed; the Marcos Díaz house; and the gaping hole made by a 500 lb bomb. Later, the students return for a poor translation of what the guides have to say. There is no question that part of the experience is hearing history from real people from El Mozote—*even if* those real people were nowhere near the area at the time of the Atlacatl operation, and *even if* most of them were born after the massacre occurred.

The first El Mozote memorial was installed in December 1991 by people from the Jesuit Central American University, who placed a metallic sculpture representing a family near the plaza site. The figures of a woman, a man, a small boy and a girl holding hands have become an iconic symbol of the massacre of entire

Figure 1. Monument to the victims (copyright Rafael Alarcón Medina)

families there. Following the December 1994 reburial of remains exhumed from the sacristy, Fa. Rogelio Ponceele oversaw the construction of the main monument adjoining the gravesite, replete with a wall, plaques containing the victims' names, a small fenced-in garden and the requisite El Mozote family. When she died in 2007, Rufina Amaya—the main witness and a tireless fighter for justice in the case—was buried, as she requested, in the garden adjacent to the main memorial. Her grave is marked by a small ceramic plate with Amaya's portrait, under which, written in golden letters, are the indefatigable words that evoke the discourse of human rights and set the El Mozote massacre alongside many other cases of state brutality and repression in Latin America: '*El Mozote nunca más*' (El Mozote never again).[20]

A few metres south of the monument lies the rebuilt Church of the Three Kings, constructed on the foundations of the former church. Until the massacre's twenty-fifth anniversary in 2006, after which Fa. Juan José del Cid assumed control from Ponceele over Catholicism there, local residents had played no role in planning annual commemorations or monuments. However, the imminent shift in religious authority led Sister Anne Griffin of the Sisters of the Sacred Hearts of Jesus and Mary, who lived in nearby Arambala, to enlist local participation in the design of a mural on the southern exterior of the church abutting the naked brick floor of the former sacristy from which Argentine forensic scientists had recovered the skeletal remains of 143 persons—seven adults and a minimum of 136 children with an average age of six years—during excavations in late 1992. This mural and another, painted on the north wall of the church by Argentine artist Claudia Bernaldi and her students, employed motifs and symbols suggested by local residents during public consultations. Though highly mediated products, the murals and accompanying Reflection Garden represent the best available evidence of the images of the past, present and future that many residents wish to project.

Blood, pain, suffering, death and destruction remain absent from these representations, particularly in the painted mural on the church's north side, which portrays the pre-war past and imagined future of El Mozote—how current residents remembered it before the war and how they would like to see the hamlet in the future.[21] The mural skips over the war and postwar period in order to portray an idealized pre-war past and a peasant utopian future. On the right side, pre-war El Mozote appears as a bucolic landscape of neatly laid out fields of corn, maguey and sugar cane with men and women hard at work cultivating crops and processing raw materials: maguey into fibre, sugar cane into *piloncillo* (semi-processed sugar). The mural offers no evidence of the poverty that compelled most people to leave the region periodically to work as cheap labour under highly oppressive conditions on capitalist plantations in agro-export zones on the coast and in the volcanic cordillera. On the left side, images of the El Mozote Hospital and Bilingual School project a desired future. The Bilingual School obliquely references international migration and the economic advantage enjoyed by migrants able to speak English. In one section of the mural, a group of young people surround a man reading a book entitled *Historia de El Mozote*, while in the centre, as if hovering over the landscape of history, a young man and young

Figure 2. El Mozote's past mural (copyright Rafael Alarcón Medina)

woman peer at a laptop computer screen upon which appear images from the mural itself. They are learning the history of El Mozote on the internet. The present of poverty, unemployment, international migration to the United States and the resulting reliance on remittances make no explicit appearance.

The Garden of Reflection-The Innocents (*Jardin de Reflexión-Los Inocentes*) lies on the south side of the church and encompasses the old sacristy site where most of the bodies of children were exhumed. The Mural of Light (*El Mural de la Luz*) on the church wall bordering the garden provides an abstract representation of death (in the massacre) and ascent to God and heaven. Children play in a field surrounded by fireflies, butterflies and stars. The left and right extremes are painted in dark blue, representing the night, the darkness of the massacre and death; towards the centre the colour transitions to green and finally to bright yellow. Abstract figures of featureless children—they could be anyone, anywhere—play merrily on the ground in the dark areas and rise ethereally as one's gaze shifts towards the

Figure 3. The 'Mural de la Luz' (copyright Rafael Alarcón Medina)

centre. A large mosaic sun has been embedded above a side door at the centre of the artwork. A guide interprets the sun as God and the rising figures as the children's souls ascending into God's hands. Brown tiles inscribed with the names and ages of the massacred children, ranging from six months to twelve years old, line the foot of the exterior wall beneath the mural. The church wall and associated mural overlook a small section of the former sacristy's brick floor, now surrounded by a small rose garden; blood stains remain visible on some of the bricks, legacies of the crimes committed there.

The guides explain the significance of the images, artefacts and references at the site, but there exists no standard narrative—despite PRODETUR's efforts to develop one—and explanations vary somewhat from one guide and time to another. Likewise, the historical facts about the massacre itself are never exactly the same, not even with the same guide. Guides may omit information, focus more on some aspects of the history than others, or even invent information and interpretations. In interviews several guides cited Rufina Amaya as their primary source, explaining that they learned the history by listening to her testimony when she accompanied international visitors to El Mozote. Others cited *Luciernagas en El Mozote* (*Fireflies in El Mozote*), a compendium of excerpts from several popular sources, including Mark Danner's work, as their principal textual source.

Tourists began to visit El Mozote even prior to its postwar repopulation,[22] but PRODETUR undertook no programme there until the first years of the new millennium, when it constructed the kiosk and helped form a woman's collective to man it and guide visitors around. Early tourism was inspired by the town's notorious reputation as the main site of brutal state repression and benefited from the international publicity given to the annual commemorations and the human rights struggles of Tutela Legal and CEBES. Later, Sister Anne carried the relationships she developed while leading the mural and garden projects into the formation of a Victim's Committee (*Comité Pro-Derechos Humanos*), which played an instrumental role in prosecuting the case internationally before the Inter-American Court of Human Rights. Prior to organizing around the mural and garden work, local inhabitants had shown little interest in the court case. Thus, social justice and not tourism per se has always been at the core of Sister Anne's work in El Mozote. Even so, the two murals and accompanying garden, laid out around the remains of the sacristy floor, form a colourful visual field replete with attractive images conducive to display in tourist brochures and on internet sites. In 2012, PRODETUR piggybacked on the popularity of El Mozote to open a 'Guacamaya Trail', hoping to persuade visitors to El Mozote to continue on to the ERP's early command post, the Bat Cave that once housed Radio Venceremos (the rebels' clandestine radio station) and a training centre.

Contested images

The El Mozote guides begin their brief tour in front of the main monument, where they explain how army troops streamed into El Mozote in mid December 1981 and found a multitude of people gathered in the plaza because Marcos Díaz had told them they would not be harmed if they assembled there. The army separated the group according to age and gender and interned them in homes overnight. The next day they took out the men and killed them in small groups and drove the younger women to the hills of Cerro Chingo and Cerro La Cruz, where soldiers raped and murdered them. The older women, enclosed in the house of Alfredo Márquez, heard the screams and covered the children's ears. In the end, the army took them, too, out to be killed. At that time Rufina Amaya escaped by crouching behind a crab-apple tree and, as night fell, she crawled into a nearby maguey field, where she waited for the army to leave town. The guides explain that Amaya, fearing that the soldiers would hear her, dug a hole in the earth, buried her face, and quietly wept for her murdered family.

The guides end with the most disturbing element of the massacre: the killing of children. Indeed, the deaths of the children are a main, dark attraction at the site, and sometimes the guides are overcome by emotion, voices quavering and eyes filled with tears. Symbolically, the children—about half the remains recovered thus far were of people estimated to have been twelve years old or less—represent the collective innocence of the massacre victims.[23] The guides explain that soldiers ripped the children from their mothers' arms and that their screams were heard by Rufina Amaya, who could identify her son's voice calling to her: 'Mama, they are killing us, they are stabbing us!' Guides sometimes recount how the soldiers threw the smallest children into the air and impaled them on knives and bayonets as they fell; others cut living foetuses from mothers' wombs and smashed them on the floor. During a visit in 2012, one guide added a new element to the story: pointing to a large tree in the Garden of Reflection, she described how after having killed the children and torn babies from their mothers' wombs the soldiers hung the small bodies from the branches of the tree like macabre Christmas ornaments. But like the stories of impalement on knives and bayonets, this story is decidedly apocryphal, sustained by no evidence, whether written, oral or forensic, collected by the EAAF, Tutela Legal, CEBES or anyone else. Its origins remain a mystery, but it seems likely that it represents the transference to the church and embellishment of a single eyewitness report, narrated by Mark Danner, of children hung from a tree near the school.[24] Some guides may hope that adding copious amounts of blood and gore to the oral rendition of the events will compensate for the lack of graphic depictions of the massacre in the mural images and encourage visitors' donations. On the other hand, the account reflects that guide's perception of the horror of the massacre and a semi-conscious integration of available elements into a plausible narrative capable of communicating that horror to visitors.

The desire on the part of some residents that El Mozote be remembered 'as it was before the war'—that nostalgia for a timeless past that never really existed as portrayed on the north wall mural—contrasts starkly with the guides' explicit narratives of rape, torture and death. Of course, people there know very well what occurred at El Mozote, but they do not want El Mozote to be known exclusively as the site of wanton death and destruction. This selective memorization is common throughout northern Morazán, even among many former guerrilla fighters, who are more likely to recall that which they lost than the little—which seems to grow in quantity and quality over time—they had to lose. One index of the conflicting and contradictory perspectives was the demand for a programme of agricultural development—the restoration of El Mozote's mythical past—as part of state reparations, precisely during a period in which privatization and free trade policies have ruined small-scale agriculture throughout the country. Many (particularly older) people in and around El Mozote would like to think of the civil war, massacre and perhaps postwar poverty and conflict as an unfortunate interregnum between two epochs, each characterized by civil peace, social harmony and economic progress—one past, the other yet to come.[25]

Guides sometimes mark the church mural as an external account that objectifies the people of El Mozote and with which they do not entirely identify: 'This mural shows how El Mozote was before the war and how people want it to be in the future'. Conflicts also exist between the women's cooperative that runs the kiosk adjacent to the museum and others who complain that the guides are 'profiting' (*lucrando*) from their work at the site, which to some very small degree they are.

The most significant conflict, however, turns around the two murals on the church's walls and draws in different wings of the Catholic Church: the inward-looking spiritualist theology of Father Juan José del Cid and the outward-looking, more politicized Liberation Theology of Father Rogelio Ponceele. According to one interviewee, Father Juan José has taken the position that the Church of the Three Kings belongs to the Catholic Church, and that as the head of the parish, he possesses the authority to destroy the murals if he wishes. He thinks that the Mural of Light depicts pagan religious ideas by identifying God with the image of the sun. During one visit to El Mozote, the Garden of Reflection was closed because the sacristan who controlled access failed to unlock the gate for guides and visitors.

Were the Church to destroy the murals, the contest over the meanings of the site and the massacre would be brought into sharper relief. Contests over the ownership and preservation of the massacre site make clear the deep political implications that the massacre has for the history of the civil war, both in northern Morazán and elsewhere. These implications become clearer when we take into consideration the role that CEBES and Father Rogelio have played in the commemorations, the murals and the movement to take the massacre case to the Inter-American Court of Human Rights. By contrast, Father Juan José cleaves close to the conservative view that the war and all that occurred during that period is best forgotten. President Alfredo Cristiani justified the 1993 Amnesty Law in precisely these terms.[26]

The struggle inside the Catholic Church in the zone—between progressive followers of Liberation Theology, albeit a more muted version than that of the 1960s and 1970s, and those who adhere to the 'traditional church'—involves a struggle around the praxis of CEBES and the ERP popular organizations during the civil war and in contemporary northern Morazán. As long as the El Mozote murals remain open to interpretation, which is to say as long as their deepest meanings remain unstable so that no one on the political right *or* left can fix their significance, they will continue to serve as a detained image of the dense time of social antagonisms there and then and here and now. Conflict over the murals' meanings serves as the social site of possibility.

The general content of the massacre site demonstrates that residents want pre-war El Mozote to be identified as a peaceful community that was the object of a savage act of irrational violence exercised upon innocent victims. Many of them used to hold the FMLN indirectly responsible for the massacre, arguing that the army would never have come to El Mozote and killed the people had the ERP not established its base nearby. A few even thought that the FMLN *committed* the massacre. Funes' acceptance of responsibility and apology quashed the latter claim and decisively weakened the former.

ERP combatants and supporters seldom pronounce on pre-war social relations in El Mozote, of which they usually had no experience, but they do agree that the people killed there had little connection to the political resistance. A short PRODETUR promotional video offers a compelling visual synthesis of the role played by the El Mozote massacre in the complex relationship that former combatants like members of PRODETUR have developed with their pasts as revolutionary fighters. The Spanish-language video, 'Peace route: where the wind whispers stories' (*Ruta de la Paz: Donde el viento susurra historias*), begins with footage of ERP Special Forces members training and a voice-over: 'It was the Salvadoran guerrillas' capital city . . . during an armed conflict that no one wanted to lose . . . Perquín, wild and beautiful land that witnessed a page of history that must not be repeated . . . if you don't recognize your history you are condemned to repeat it . . . Peace Route, Perquín, Morazán in El Salvador'.[27]

The film includes three intertwined themes: the first pertains to guerrilla military capacities, weaponry and skills with a specific visual reference to Domingo Monterrosa's helicopter and his assassination in 1984;[28] the second focuses on the zone's natural beauty; and the third takes up the El Mozote massacre, with images of the monument to the victims and the Mural of Light. The video ends with Oscar, a former guerrilla who now works as a guide, saying: 'And the idea, we say, is that arms are not the solution, and that [the] solution should be by means of dialogue'.[29]

This video portrays in broad strokes the contradictory memory of many former guerrilla fighters, who still value the struggle and are proud of what they accomplished, yet have become convinced that taking up arms is no substitute for dialogue and the rule of law. The Peace Route eschews insurgent revolutionary action for a peace built through capitalistic economic development by means of ecological and historical tourism spiced with the discourse of human rights. In the PRODETUR video, the El Mozote massacre stands for the innocent victims of an irrational violence, a 'madness' (*locura*) in the words of the 1994 Truth Commission report. The exploitation and state repression that caused the war and the collective structures and solidarity created by the FMLN and organizations linked to it during the conflict are left out. Guerrilla fighters and CEBES members are dismissed as simply a part of the madness, for which reason they do not seem to deserve a history. By contrast, the people massacred in El Mozote do have a past, even if it is, in many ways, a mythical one: they were hardworking people, who belonged to the evangelical church—not guerrillas, not mad or crazy, but innocents. Under this logic, their suffering deserves to be recognized and they are worthy of material and symbolic reparations from the state.

Based on interviews in Perquín, Torola, San Fernando and Segundo Montes City and attendance at Perquín's August 2011 Winter Festival, the El Mozote massacre has become a strong political referent for former combatants and FMLN supporters, including many young people. One of the main activities during the festival involves a commemorative walk from Perquín over Cerro Pericón to El Mozote plaza, passing other civil war-era sites along the way. Alarcón's interviewees have no doubt about the political conservatism of the people who repopulated El Mozote, but that has not stopped them from attending the commemoration that takes place there each December.

Many former ERP combatants and FMLN supporters in northern Morazán still await official recognition for their role in the popular struggle that helped bring changes for everybody in El Salvador. Even in cases where people did not explicitly articulate these thoughts, their references to the collective fruits of their labour, the price they paid, the psychological wounds and the blood of relatives lost implicitly suggest that El Salvador is a more democratic place because of their struggle. Despite the limits of this 'democracy', we believe they are right.[30] But political polarization after the civil war, the conditions of the peace accords and the unabated rule of the political right until the electoral triumph of the FMLN with Mauricio Funes in 2009 limited historical recognition of the deep social and economic roots of insurgent action. Under the peace accords' hegemonic discourse of human rights (with the Truth Commission as its main artefact), guerrilla fighters and the insurgent movement were put on a par with the army and the repressive security forces. In the end, all shared, albeit in very different proportions, a certain amount of responsibility for the dark days of El Salvador's recent violent past. Again, *la locura*.

For former ERP combatants and FMLN supporters, the El Mozote massacre has become a contradictory lens through which they symbolically articulate their demands for the recognition of state violence in Morazán during the civil war. By focusing on El Mozote, they avoid the stigmatization of their wartime activities. Thus the massacre as a historical event—and now as a memorial site—is a contested place on which contemporary social antagonisms related with the struggle around the right path towards economic development (cooperatives and solidarity or individual entrepreneurship) can be safely expressed.[31] Former combatants like the PRODETUR members have incorporated the El Mozote massacre as an important part of human rights discourse and a cornerstone of the Peace Route marketing campaign. For them, marketing northern Morazán means marketing memory too.[32] The obligatory visit to the El Mozote massacre site and its place in the promotional video express just that logic. However, given the rudimentary tourism infrastructure, northern Morazán's remote location and savage competition for the tourist dollar, it is highly doubtful that tourism development there will become a sustainable activity that will improve people's lives in the foreseeable future.

Finally, a new Peace Monument (*Monumento a la Paz*) is currently being built in El Mozote. Neither the community at large (the survivors and their families) nor organizations like CEBES have had anything to do with this initiative, which was conceived by a German priest living in Ecuador, constructed on land owned by a Salvadoran priest born in El Mozote but residing in Elizabeth, New Jersey, designed by an Ecuadorean architect and executed by an Irish Catholic volunteer engineer. Locals 'participate' as paid construction day labourers on the monument and the restaurant, museum and office buildings of what will become a reconciliation centre and religious (mainly Catholic) retreat. A reproduction of the sculpture of the family from the El Mozote massacre memorial site crowning the fourteen-metre-high monument, which dominates the immediate landscape, offers the only reference to the massacre.

The main role is played by four sculptured and painted fibreglass statues representing different religious figures symbolizing non-violence, reconciliation and peace: Mother Theresa, John Paul II, Martin Luther King and Gandhi or, as one interviewee told Alarcón: 'Mother Theresa, Jean Paul II, a brown-skinned evangelical man and the guy who sits' (*la Madre Teresa, Juan Pablo Segundo, un moreno evangélico y el señor que se sienta*). People in El Mozote are not even familiar with all those represented in the monument, though they will in all likelihood soon learn to identify them. When Alarcón asked someone involved in the monument's construction about what people in El Mozote think about the site, he replied: 'It has brought a lot of work and most of the people are content'. Work, salaries, tourism, development. The construction will continue for at least one more year, during which time the people in El Mozote and the surrounding region will grapple with the meaning of this new monument and how it transmogrifies the physical and historical landscape of their history.

Figure 4. The 'Monumento a la Paz' (copyright Rafael Alarcón Medina)

Figure 5. Statues in the 'Monumento a la Paz': John Paul II, Mother Theresa, Gandhi and Martin Luther King (copyright Rafael Alarcón Medina)

Constellations of social struggles: memory interpellation and the suspended time of praxis in northern Morazán

Today, former ERP combatants recall the massacre as a way of mediating their search for economic development through the discourses of tourism, human rights (Peace Route) and the marketing of history. Confronting its diminishing strength in local social and political fields, CEBES invested minimal resources to organize the El Mozote massacre victims' committee and to promote the case in the international legal arena. In this version of El Salvador's history, people from El Mozote play the passive role of innocent victims. In reality, many have taken an active part—albeit prodded at first—in human rights struggles and actively pursue their own economic interests by attempting to extract reparations from the state through the courts. And of course, there is also the state's political interest in controlling the meaning of El Mozote, one more battle in the endless contest over the place of the civil war in El Salvador's history. As a socially produced space, El Mozote is situated at the intersection of multiple conflicts, even as it has itself become a condensed symbol for those same processes. Thus, it can be argued that in Morazán and elsewhere, the El Mozote massacre has become transformed into a dialectical image through which people produce a contradictory consciousness of class subjectivity, derived from the historical defeat of radical popular struggle and the ideological and material pressure produced by the deepening of neoliberal political economy in El Salvador and its spread across northern Morazán.[33]

In El Mozote, much discourse on memory originates from outside the region, as an external interpellation on the parts of diverse actors to which survivors and victims' relatives respond and will continue to respond in years to come. It remains a task to investigate and understand the particular ways in which people in and around El Mozote find their place and praxis in such a process. Taking off from Walter Benjamin, we might say that memory there works as the interpellation of history, that is, as the suspended time of social antagonisms not resolved before, during and after the war. As they strive to survive and in some cases deal with their stigmatization, those Morazanians who sided with the FMLN in the armed struggle look to the El Mozote massacre as a key symbolic referent through which they convey, obliquely to be sure, their demands to the state for material and symbolic reparations and economic development. The dead at El Mozote stand in for or represent countless others in Morazán and elsewhere whose deaths have gone unrecorded and unnoticed. This is one of the attractions of the site for many Salvadorans, symbolized by the featureless children in the Mural of Light.

The recognition of the massacre by the Salvadoran state is, without doubt, an important step after thirty years of silence and impunity, first under the rule of the military and later the ultra-conservative ARENA party. But the discourse of innocence attached to the El Mozote massacre presents a roadblock to the acknowledgement of the role of popular struggle in the history of El Salvador for it effects ignorance of the very real choices made by those who died there—their allegiance to the government and trust in the army—and tacitly discredits others who rebelled. In this discourse, only the innocent, the passive, the politically neutral (itself the product of choice) merit consideration. The ERP-FMLN committed abuses and made numerous mistakes, yet the fact remains that thousands of Morazanians risked their lives in the war, many of them inspired by a utopian ideal of social justice. The popular armed struggle was not *a locura* but the outcome of decades of socioeconomic injustice, militarization and oligarchic repression.[34]

Working on Benjamin's theses on history, we propose to think of memory as the actualization, in an instant, of what appears to be detained. Benjamin argues that in the history of popular struggle, what is always detained in memory is praxis as the concrete possibilities of articulated intervention by the working classes in history.[35] It is the clarity of the active and conscious participation and control of the material and symbolic (re)production of everyday life, something that the former combatants and FMLN supporters glimpsed during the civil war through the solidary forms of organization they developed, but which many have forgotten or remember from the perspective of a present configured by two decades of relentless assault on and criticism of collective organization and glorification of the market and individualism.[36] This time detention comprises the density of social time, what Benjamin called the *Jetzt-zeit* (time-now), the different temporalities embodied by the complex web of disarticulated popular struggles and demands in northern Morazán. Memory as the suspended time of praxis involves the presence of older struggles through an image that can, at some point, articulate the past with the present. We believe that the El Mozote massacre is such a contradictory image: a dialectical image that weaves together two different historical constellations, the past and present of people in northern Morazán.[37] However, memory can also be transformed into an emergent form of historical synthesis (as memorialization) in which the density of past and present antagonisms is erased under the empty and linear time of capitalistic modernity and its forms of social history. The standardization of the massacre narrative, in an effort to more effectively market the history of a purportedly harmonious 'community' destroyed for no rational reason—the inhabitants were after all 'Evangelicals'—erases the paradigmatic chain of relationships that tied people in El Mozote and the surrounding region to one another, El Mozote and northern Morazán to agro-export zones and El Salvador (then and now) to the United States.[38] The recognition of the massacre by the Salvadoran state under the discourses of human rights and innocence can further this erasure; a settlement of the demands vis-à-vis symbolic and material reparations would represent yet another step in that direction. Through the official discourse, '*El Mozote nunca más*' could become '*Revolución nunca más*'. Again, *la locura*.[39]

El Mozote is being marketed by PRODETUR and others on the back of human rights discourse. But the political and civil rights that such discourse normally upholds elide the silent, 'invisible' everyday forms of violence generated by institutionalized social and economic inequalities.[40] These forms of structural violence are more common than ever; successfully combating them requires organized social movements, but such movements risk being displaced by human rights discourse and practice if the latter gains a hegemonic position.[41] Those who understand the war as a *locura* that ended in peace, free speech, elections, the demilitarization of the police force and even a Human Rights Ombudsman forget that it did not improve the material life of most Salvadorans. As so often occurs under transitional justice, wealthy and powerful oligarchs and their allies who benefited from exploitation and oppression before and during the war have been allowed to keep their gains; with few legal options to attain a dignified life in El Salvador, a growing number of poor people imagine their future in the United States, which has unofficially become El Salvador's 'fifteenth department'.[42] In repeated interviews during the summers of 2010–2012, former rebel fighters and their supporters lauded the increase in postwar political freedoms but characterized economic improvements as '*pendiente*' (pending). Debate and discussion about the war and events therein—causes, meanings and implications for the future—are thus needed more than ever. In his fifth thesis on history, Walter Benjamin stated that 'every image of the past that is not recognized by the present as one of its own concerns threatens to disappear irretrievably'.[43]

Occupying a marginal place in the mural about El Mozote's past, one element is sometimes overlooked in the guides' narratives. When Alarcón asked about it, a guide told him, 'Ah ... that is the Angel of History'. As Benjamin suggests, there rests in each of us a small messianic force. In El Mozote, the massacre is a dialectical image with a contradictory strength of redemption waiting to blow up the continuum of history. It is the suspended time of a praxis that waits to break into time as social struggle, exploding the empty and linear time of capitalist society that pretends that nothing ever really happens. As Tabare Etcheverry's song, quoted at the beginning of this article, says: '*Pa´llorar por los que han muerto somos todos muy valientes, pa´llorar por los que han muerto siempre hay muchísima gente*' (To cry for those who have died we are all too brave; to cry for those who have died, there are always too many people). To condemn violence, repression and human rights abuses there are always too many people. However—and in this case the Truth Commission got it right—*morir por los pueblos es cosa de locos, para 'morir por los pueblos hay muy pocos'* (To die for the pueblos is crazy people stuff; to die for the pueblos there are always very few). Former ERP combatants, people from CEBES and many of the participants in the civil war, combatants and civilians alike, fought and died so that the people in El Salvador can have now a little more liberty. Their continued struggles contain the final meaning of the El Mozote massacre for contemporary postwar El Salvador.

Acknowledgements

We acknowledge the financial support of the National Science Foundation for supporting 'From wartime to peacetime: post-insurgent individuality in northern Morazán, El Salvador', grant No. BCS 0962643 (Ellen Moodie, PI, Leigh Binford co-PI), which made it possible for us to carry out much of the ethnographic work on which this article is based. In addition, Alarcón acknowledges the Consejo Nacional de Ciencia y Tecnología of México for its financial support (grant #33743).

Endnotes

1 'To cry for those who have died, we are all too brave; to cry for those who have died, there are always too many people; but to die for the 'pueblos' (popular classes) is crazy people stuff; to die for the pueblos, there are always very few; and we look for the guilty when a brave man is killed, and we look for the guilty when an innocent dies; it was not the killers, it was us who let them die for being so few'. Extract from '*Cuzco rabón*' by Tabaré Etcheverry (1945–1978), a popular Uruguayan singer and songwriter. Available at http://acordes.lacuerda.net/tabare_etcheverry/por_ser_tan_pocos.shtml (retrieved 10 August 2014).

2 Funes won the presidency in 2009 on the FMLN ticket but is not a member of the party. The FMLN victory followed three failed postwar attempts (1994, 1999 and 2004) to capture the presidency.

3 Corte Interamericana de Derechos Humanos (CIDH), 'Case Masacres de El Mozote y lugares aledaños vs. El Salvador', Sentence of 25 October 2012. Available at http://www.corteidh.or.cr/des/casos/articulos/seriec_252_esp.pdf.

4 Mark Danner, *The massacre at El Mozote* (New York: Vintage Books, 1994).

5 Danner, *The massacre at El Mozote*, p. 19.

6 CIDH, 'Masacres de El Mozote y lugares aledaños, El Salvador', Caso No. 10.720, 8 March de 2011.

7 Leigh Binford, *The El Mozote massacre: anthropology and human rights* (Tucson: University of Arizona Press, 1996); see also Stener Ekern, 'The modernizing bias of human rights: stories of mass killings and genocide in Central America', *Journal of Genocide Research*, Vol. 12, No. 3, 2010, pp. 219–241.

8 Binford, *The El Mozote massacre*, pp. 68–89.

9 Danner, *The massacre at El Mozote*; Raymond Bonner, 'Massacre of hundreds reported in Salvador village', *New York Times*, 27 January 1982; Carlos Henríquez Consalvi (Santiago), *La terquedad del Izote. La historia de Radio Venceremos* (El Salvador: Museo de la Palabra y la Imagen, 2002).

10 SOA Watch, 'The dead: victims at El Mozote and nearby villages', available at: http://soaw.org/index.php?option=com_content&view=article&id=43 (retrieved 8 June 2014).

11 Elizabeth Jelin, *State repression and the labors of memory* (Minneapolis: University of Minnesota Press, 2003).

12 During the summers of 2010–2012, the authors, along with Dr. Ellen Moodie, carried out participant observation in El Mozote on numerous occasions. They also conducted more than a dozen formal interviews with members of CEBES, Sister Anne, current residents and others. El Mozote also came up in many interviews carried out with former ERP combatants and their supporters as part of the larger National Science Foundation-supported project.

13 José Inocencio Alas, *Iglesia, tierra y lucha campesina. Suchitoto, El Salvador, 1968–1977* (El Salvador: Equipo Maíz, 2003); Carlos Rafael Cabarrús, *Génesis de una revolución: análisis del surgimiento y desarrollo de la organización campesina en El Salvador* (México: CIESAS, 1983).

14 María López Vigil, *Death and life in Morazán: a priest's testimony from a war-zone in El Salvador* (London: Catholic Institute for International Relations, 1989).

15 Michael McClintock, *The American connection: state terror and popular resistance in El Salvador* (London: Zed Books, 1985); José Ignacio López Vigil, *Rebel radio: the story of El Salvador's Radio Venceremos* (Willimantic, CT: Curbstone Press, 1995); Cecilia Menjívar and Néstor Rodríguez, *When states kill: Latin America, the US and technologies of terror* (Austin: University of Texas Press, 2005); Gilbert Joseph and Greg Grandin, *In from the cold: Latin America's new encounter with the Cold War* (Durham: Duke University Press, 2008).

16 Leigh Binford, 'Hegemony in the interior of the Salvadoran revolution: the ERP in northern Morazán', *Journal of Latin American Anthropology*, Vol. 4, No. 1, 1999, pp. 2–45.

17 Leigh Binford, 'A perfect storm of neglect and failure: postwar capitalist restoration in northern Morazán, El Salvador', *Journal of Peasant Studies*, Vol. 37, No. 3, 2010, pp. 531–557; Mandy Macdonald and Mike Gatehouse, *In the mountains of Morazan: portrait of a returned refugee community in El Salvador* (New York: Monthly Review Press, 1995).

18 Ellen Moodie, *El Salvador in the aftermath of peace: crime, uncertainty, and the transition to democracy* (Philadelphia: University of Pennsylvania Press, 2010); Mo Hume, *The politics of violence: gender, conflict and community in El Salvador* (Malden, MA and Oxford: Wiley-Blackwell, 2009).

19 Leigh Binford, 'Ecotourism, migration and historical memory in northern Morazán, El Salvador', in Jennifer Burrell and Ellen Moodie (eds.), *Central America in the new millennium: living transition and reimagining democracy* (New York: Berghahn Books, 2013), pp. 245–260.

20 'Never Again' served as the title of the 1984 report of the Argentine National Commission on the Disappearance of Persons (Comisión Nacional sobre la Desaparición de Personas, CONADEP), and according to Bilbija and Payne became adopted far beyond Argentina as 'the slogan for the purposeful action of remembering past atrocity'. Ksenija Bilbija and Leigh A. Payne, 'Introduction: time is money: the memory market in Latin America', in Ksenija Bilbija and Leigh A. Payne (eds.), *Accounting for violence: marketing memory in Latin America* (Durham: Duke University Press, 2011), p. 15.

21 Claudia Bernaldi, 'Whispers at El Mozote', *Peace Review*, Vol. 22, No. 3, 2010, pp. 250–252.

22 Binford, 'A perfect storm'.

23 Equipo Argentino de Antropología Forense (EAAF), 'Informe arqueológico' in Naciones Unidas, *Informe de la comisión de la verdad* (San Salvador, 1993).

24 Danner, *The massacre at El Mozote*, p. 77. Danner cites 'Chepe Mozote' to the effect that on a playing field next to the school, the soldiers 'slit some of the kids' throats, and many they hanged from the tree'.

25 Equipo Maíz, *La composición social de El Salvador* (San Salvador: Asociación Equipo Maíz, 2009).

26 The FMLN Party did not oppose the Amnesty Law for the Consolidation of Peace, since the law shielded the leadership from potential prosecution for wartime human rights violations. See Alexander Segovia, 'Transitional justice and DDR: the case of El Salvador', International Center for Transitional Justice, 2009, available at: www.ictj.org//sites/default/files/ITCJ-DDR-ElSalvador-CaseStudy-2009-English.pdf (retrieved 17 May 2013).

27 All translations from Spanish are by the authors.

28 Monterrosa was reputedly killed in a helicopter explosion, the product of a sophisticated ERP Trojan Horse operation designed to take advantage of the colonel's penchant for collecting war trophies and his rabid desire to capture Radio Venceremos. See López Vigil, *Rebel radio*.

29 https://www.youtube.com/watch?v=oDmXb2kFK8M.

30 Sonja Wolf, 'Subverting democracy: elite rule and the limits to political participation in post-war El Salvador', *Journal of Latin American Studies*, Vol. 41, No. 3, 2009, pp. 429–465.

31 Binford, 'A perfect storm', pp. 554–555.

32 See Bilbija and Payne, 'Introduction'.

33 Walter Benjamin, 'Theses on the philosophy of history', in Walter Benjamin (ed.), *Illuminations* (New York, Schocken, 1968), pp. 253–264; Benjamin, *One-way street and other writings* (London: Penguin Books, 2009).
34 Sara Gordon, *Crisis política y guerra en El Salvador* (Mexico: Siglo XXI, 1989); Aldo Laura-Santiago, 'The culture and politics of state terror and repression in El Salvador' in Cecelia Menjivar and Néstor Rodríguez, eds., When states kill: Latin America, the US and technologies of terror (Austin, TX: University of Texas Press, 2005), pp. 85–114; Patricia Alvarenga, *Cultura y ética de la violencia. El Salvador 1880–1932* (El Salvador: CONCULTURA, 2006); James Dunkerley, *Power in the isthmus* (London: Verso, 1989); Jeffrey Gould and Aldo Lauria-Santiago, *1932. Rebelión en la oscuridad* (El Salvador: Museo de la Palabra y la Imagen, 2008).
35 Benjamin, 'Theses on the philosophy of history', pp. 254–255.
36 See Cabarrús, *Génesis de una revolución*; Minor Sinclair, *The new politics of survival. Grassroots movements in Central America* (New York: Monthly Review Press, 1995); Francisco Metzi, *Por los caminos de Chalatenango: con la salud en la mochila* (El Salvador: Universidad Centroamericana, 1988); Lucio Vázquez (Chiyo), *Siete gorriones* (El Salvador: Museo de la Palabra y la Imagen, 2012); Elizabeth Jean Wood, *Insurgent collective action and civil war in El Salvador* (Cambridge: Cambridge University Press, 2003); Irina Carlota Silber, *Everyday revolutionaries: gender, violence, and disillusionment in postwar El Salvador* (New Brunswick: Rutgers University Press, 2010).
37 Benjamin, 'Theses on the philosophy of history', p. 255.
38 David Pedersen, *American value: migrants, money and meaning in El Salvador and the United States* (Chicago: University of Chicago Press, 2013).
39 See Greg Grandin and Thomas Miller Klubock, 'Editor's introduction', *Radical History Review*, Vol. 97, 2007, pp. 1–10; Nora Strejilevich, 'Performative memorial sites and resistance in Argentina', *Peace Review*, Vol. 22, No. 3, 2010, pp. 236–243; Antonius Robben, 'From dirty war to genocide: Argentina's resistance to national reconciliation', *Memory Studies*, Vol. 5, No. 3, 2012, pp. 305–315; Katrien Klep, 'Tracing collective memory: Chilean truth commissions and memorial sites', *Memory Studies*, Vol. 5, No. 3, 2012, pp. 259–269; Ann Rigney, 'Reconciliation and remembering: (how) does it work?', *Memory Studies*, Vol. 5, No. 3, 2012, pp. 251–258.
40 Rosemary Nagy, 'Transitional justice as global project: critical reflections', *Third World Quarterly*, Vol. 29, No. 2, 2008, pp. 275–289; Rama Mani, 'Editorial: dilemmas of expanding transitional justice, or forging the nexus between transitional justice and development', *International Journal of Transitional Justice*, Vol. 2, 2008, pp. 253–265.
41 Wendy Brown, 'The most we can hope for: human rights and the politics of fatalism', *South Atlantic Quarterly*, Vol. 103, Nos. 2–3, 2004, pp. 451–463.
42 Robert Meister, 'Human rights and the politics of victimhood', *Ethics & International Affairs*, Vol. 16, No. 2, 2002, pp. 91–108; Cecelia M. Rivas, 'Tracing the borderless in "Departamento 15"', in Cecilia M. Rivas (ed.), *Salvadoran imaginaries: mediated identities and cultures of consumption* (New Brunswick: Rutgers University Press, 2014), pp. 19–48.
43 Benjamin, 'Theses on the philosophy of history', pp. 253–264.

Index

For Product Safety Concerns and Information please contact our EU representative GPSR@taylorandfrancis.com Taylor & Francis Verlag GmbH, Kaufingerstraße 24, 80331 München, Germany

Batch number: 10726294

Printed by Printforce, the Netherlands